SERIES EDITOR: TONY HOLMES

OSPREY AVIATION

B-29 Hu...
of the JAAF

Koji Takaki & Henry Sakaida

OSPREY
PUBLISHING

Front cover
'Kato, let's go in!' were the last words spoken by 2Lt Osamu Hirose, pilot of a 53rd Sentai's Ki-45 *Toryu*, on 19 February 1945 as he dived into the nose of Capt Stanley H Samuelson's B-29 42-24692 of the 500th BG. This ramming took place east of Mt Fuji at an altitude of 28,500 ft, and the only survivors of the collision were Hirose's observer, Cpl Kimio Kato, and B-29 radar operator S/Sgt Robert P Evans – fellow crewman Robert Janecek also survived the collision but was badly burned, and he later died on 6 March from a lack of medical attention. Mission 37 to Tokyo, flown by the 73rd and 313th BWs, cost them six B-29s, two of which were rammed (*Cover artwork by Jim Laurier*)

First published in Great Britain in 2001 by Osprey Publishing
Elms Court, Chapel Way, Botley, Oxford, OX2 9LP

ISBN 1 84176 161 3

Edited by Tony Holmes and Neil Maxwell
Page design by Mark Holt
Cover Artwork by Jim Laurier
Aircraft Profiles and Badge Artwork by Jim Laurier and Mark Styling
Origination by Grasmere Digital Imaging, Leeds, UK
Printed through Bookbuilders, Hong Kong

00 01 02 03 04   10 9 8 7 6 5 4 3 2 1

ACKNOWLEDGEMENTS
The Authors wish to thank the following individuals for their help – F J Bradley, Tom Britton, John M Campbell, Len Chaloux, Bill Copeland, 'Sparky' Corradina, Josh Curtis, Toru Fukubayashi, Haruyoshi Furukawa, Hap Halloran, Dr Yasuho Izawa, Walter Huss, Masao Katoh, Masaji Kobayashi, Satohide Kohatsu, Yasuo Kumoi, Chester Marshall, David Maxwell, Kiyoko Ogata, Kazuhiko Osuo and Sallyann Wagoner.

AUTHORS' NOTE
Readers wishing to learn more about the B-29 Superfortress are encouraged to visit the following website devoted to its legacy at – http://b-29.org/

EDITOR'S NOTE
To make this new series as authoritative as possible, the Editor would be interested in hearing from any individual who may have relevant photographs, documentation or first-hand experiences relating to the world's elite units, their aircraft Force, and the crews that flew them, in the various theatres of war. Any material used will be credited to its original source. Please write to Tony Holmes at 10 Prospect Road, Sevenoaks, Kent, TN13 3UA, Great Britain, or by e-mail at: tony.holmes@osprey-jets.freeserve.co.uk

For details of all Osprey Publishing titles please contact us at:

Osprey Direct UK, P.O. Box 140, Wellingborough, Northants NN8 4ZA, UK
E-mail: **info@ospreydirect.co.uk**

Osprey Direct USA, P.O. Box 130, Sterling Heights, MI 48311-0130, USA
E-mail: **info@ospreydirectusa.com**

Or visit our website: **www.ospreypublishing.com**

CONTENTS

JAAF VERSUS THE 58th BW

By 1944 the war had turned against the Japanese. And with the introduction of the Boeing B-29 Superfortress into the China-Burma-India (CBI) theatre, Japan's fate was sealed. XX Bomber Command sent the 58th Bombardment Wing (BW) to India to establish a rear base. From Calcutta, it would move to forward airfields in Chengtu, China, which were within striking distance of the Japanese mainland.

The Japanese High Command was aware of the new B-29s thanks to reports from the JAAF's 64th Sentai (air group), based in Burma, and the first skirmish was not long in coming. Capt Hideo Miyabe, commander of this famous fighter unit, was the first Japanese to attack the Superfortress, in a joint operation with the 204th Sentai.

On 26 April 1944, B-29 No 42-6330 of the 444th Bombardment Group (BG), piloted by Maj Charles Hansen, was at 16,000 ft over the China/India border when it was attacked by Ki-43 'Oscars'. During the half-hour engagement that followed, the B-29's top turret and 20 mm tail cannon failed, and Sgt Walter Gilonski, who was manning a side gun, was wounded. However, tail gunner Sgt Harold Lanahan, who was able to clear his twin 0.50-cal machine guns, thought he had scored a kill.

Meanwhile, Miyabe reported shooting out the B-29's right engine, and the Japanese claimed the aircraft was destroyed. As it happens, the B-29 went on its way with eight holes in it, while the Japanese pilots turned for home without any losses.

Intelligence in Tokyo correctly surmised that once the Americans had reached their forward bases in China, Japan could expect raids on its factories in northern Kyushu from across the East China Sea. Japanese commanders also believed the first attack would come at night, but not before the Americans had solved their supply problems.

B-29s, C-109s (converted B-24 tankers) and C-47 transports of the Air Transport Command made more than 1400 trips over the 'Hump', as the Himalayas were known, to bring supplies into China. Early-model B-29s had been stripped down to be used as bulk fuel carriers, and by June 1944 the Americans had amassed enough fuel, ordnance, supplies, aircrew and aircraft to take the war to the heart of enemy territory.

At 1616 hrs on 15 June, the first of the 58th BW's 68 B-29s took to the air from the wing's bases at Chengtu. Each aircraft carried a payload of only two tons for the mission, which saw the 58th targeting steel factories at Yawata, on the northern coast of Kyushu Island. Since the operation was very long-range, and fuel conservation was critical, it had been decided that each aircraft would make its own way to the target rather than fly in massed formations. Altitude would be between 8500-11,000 ft.

If the Americans were expecting the raid to be a surprise, they were mistaken, for Japanese army observers in China were quick to report the unusual air activity they had detected to the Western Air Defence Command in Fukuoka, on the Japanese mainland. Early-warning radar on Cheju Island, off the south coast of Korea in the East China Sea, had picked up large numbers of aircraft.

Lt Tom Friedman, flying with the 40th BG as a radar counter-measures technician, listened on his equipment for signs of Japanese radar. A strong whining signal through his analyser told him they were being 'painted';

'We had been detected well back of the Chinese coast, and several hours from the target. As we neared the coast other signals came and increased in strength. It was an eerie feeling to know that far below, our every move was being carefully watched on scopes and plotting boards.'

The Japanese issued orders to scramble. That honour fell to the 4th Sentai, based at Ozuki airfield in western Honshu, and it would be the first unit to engage the Superfortresses over Japan. The 4th Sentai had briefly taken part in the invasion of the Philippines at the beginning of the war, and in January 1942 had returned to Ozuki for home defence duties over northern Kyushu.

The 4th was equipped with the twin-engined Kawasaki Ki-45 *Toryu* ('Dragon Slayer'). Codenamed 'Nick', the aircraft had been designed as a long-range fighter, but had failed to live up to expectations. However, it excelled in the ground-attack and nightfighter roles, the latter variant boasting a service ceiling of 10,000 m (32,810 ft) and a maximum speed of 540 kmh at 6000 m (335 mph at 19,685 ft). At this stage only eight

Pilots and observers of the 3rd Chutai/4th Sentai salute their CO, Capt Masaji Kobayashi, at Ozuki airfield in January 1944. In the background are twin-engined 'Nicks'. The men were undergoing nightfighter training at the time (*Maru*)

Capt Masaji Kobayashi holds a model of a Flying Fortress which he used to instruct his men. They also trained with the real thing, for the unit was supplied with an airworthy B-17E that had been captured in Java in early 1942. As the Americans set up their forward bases in China, the Japanese correctly deduced that the B-29s would attack northern Kyushu (*M Kobayashi*)

aircraft had been converted for nightfighting, six of these carrying conventional armaments of 20 mm and 13 mm guns, and two equipped with 37 mm cannon.

Expecting the enemy to attack under the cover of darkness, the unit began training its pilots in the specialised skills of nightfighting. Of its 40 pilots, only 15 were qualified to fly at night, and most of these had completed more than 500 hours of training.

To work out its tactics, the unit used a captured B-17E taken at Bandung, Java, in early 1942. Attacking the target head-on and from above was the method decided on, and aside from practising with the Flying Fortress, the unit also employed towed target banners as pilots familiarised themselves with performing co-ordinated attacks in conjunction with ground searchlight units.

Meanwhile, as the Superfortresses lumbered towards Yawata, the 4th Sentai scrambled 24 'Nicks' in flights of four aircraft. It did not matter that many of the pilots had completed only half their night training – they

were thrown into the fighting along with the few veterans. They were in for a shock. To see the massive B-29 for the first time would have been an horrific experience for any home defence pilot. In his memoir, 1Lt Isamu Kashiide recorded his first impression of the mighty aircraft;

'I was flying over the industrial area of northern Kyushu. The unit commander gave the order "Enemy planes invading an important area! Every flight attack!" At the same time, ground searchlights in the area lit up the sky.

'Finally I sighted an enemy four-engined bomber. I was scared! It was known that the B-29 was a huge plane, but when I saw my opponent it was much larger than I had ever expected. There was no question that when compared with the B-17, the B-29 was indeed the "Superfortress"! The figure that appeared in the searchlight made me think of a great whale in the ocean. I was just astounded by its size.'

Sixty-two B-29s arrived at their destination, and at 2338 hrs (China time) they began dropping their 500-lb GP (general purpose) bombs. Due to 5/10ths cloud cover and a blackout over Yawata, only 15 Superfortresses bombed visually, while others dropped by radar – only one bomb landed on the intended target. Meanwhile, bomber crewmen reported that enemy attacks were weak, with only 12 passes being made within 500 yards. The B-29 gunners made no claims.

However, ineffective as the Japanese tactics might have seemed, the Americans did not return home unscathed, with *Limber Dugan* (42-6230) of the 468th BG becoming the first B-29 to be shot down over Japan. The successful pilot was WO Sadamitsu Kimura, who caught the Superfortress in the searchlights from below and started to attack.

'I approached it to within 20 or 30 metres', he recounted in the July 1944 edition of aviation magazine *Koku Shonen* (Flying Youth). 'Suddenly, everything became white because of the reflected light off the big fuselage of the enemy plane, which filled my gunsight. It started to climb in fear of being rammed by me. I did not hesitate! I started to fire, and I could tell that I hit it. The nose came down slowly and it started to spin. I saw one piece of the fin come off'.

The 58th BW lost a total of seven B-29s on the mission. However, only one was shot down and six were operational losses. Flak damaged six others.

In their first nightfighting sortie, which lasted two hours, the pilots of the 4th Sentai claimed seven B-29s shot down and six damaged – over-enthusiasm which can be put down to a combination of darkness and confusion. Nevertheless, 28-year-old Sadamitsu Kimura was Japan's hero of the night. He claimed to have shot down three B-29s, and for his feats of

1Lt Isamu Kashiide combs through the wreckage of *Limber Dugan* of the 468th BG (*Y Kumoi*)

Another view of the wreckage of *Limber Dugan*. This aircraft was shot down over Wakamatsu, in northern Kyushu, by 2Lt Sadamitsu Kimura, flying a Ki-45 (*Y Kumoi*)

daring was awarded a military sword from Army Minister Gen Hideki Tojo. The other supposed 'kills' were claimed by 1Lt Kashiide (two) and Capt Masaji Kobayashi and WO Hannoshin Nishio (one each). Only one 'Nick' was hit and damaged.

As far as the JAAF was concerned, the 37 mm cannon, and the pilots using them had proved themselves, especially considering the gun's limitations and lack of available ammunition. Isamu Kashiide commented;

'Our plane's nose was reconstructed to accommodate the gun, but it was limited and could only carry 15 rounds. The rate of fire was three shots

Pilots of the 4th Sentai are interviewed by a newspaper reporter (back towards camera) on the afternoon of 16 June 1944. The previous night B-29s from the 58th BW had raided northern Kyushu, and men from this sentai had attempted to repel them over Yawata. They are clockwise, Capt Masaji Kobayashi, Maj Isao Abe (CO of the unit), Chief of Staff of the 19th Air Brigade, 1Lt Isamu Kashiide, WO Sadamitsu Kimura and Capt Toshio Sassa (*Y Watanabe*)

These five pilots of the 4th Sentai would make names for themselves in the battles against the B-29s. Standing, left to right, are Sgts Shigeo Nobe, Hannoshin Nishio and Shinji Mori. Sitting, left to right, are Sgt Minoru Uchida and 1Lt Isamu Kashiide (*via H Sakaida*)

11

1Lt Isamu Kashiide in his high-altitude flying gear – the fur-lined suit was electrically heated. In his post-war memoir, Kashiide claimed an incredible 26 B-29 victories, plus seven kills against the Soviets in the 1939 border skirmish at Nomonhan. His B-29 tally is disputed by his former colleagues and historians, and his true score is believed to be around seven (*via H Sakaida*)

per minute. Unlike the machine gun, it could not be freely manipulated. Sadly lacking were essential war supplies. "One shot, one kill" became our attitude. Every shot had to count.'

FIRST RAMMING ATTACK

On 20 August, four groups from XX Bomber Command (40th, 444th, 462nd and 468th), comprising 76 aircraft, took off from their bases in China. They were led by Col Howard Engler, commander of the 468th, with Brig Gen Saunders, the strike commander, coming along to observe. Each B-29 carried one-and-a-half tons of 500-lb GPs intended for the iron and steel factories at Yawata.

Within minutes of take-off the Japanese were alerted, for once again the early-warning radar stations had detected the approach of massed formations. At 1632 hrs the Western Air Defence Command put out a warning of an air raid, and the Japanese army's 4th, 51st, 52nd and 59th Sentais were scrambled to intercept.

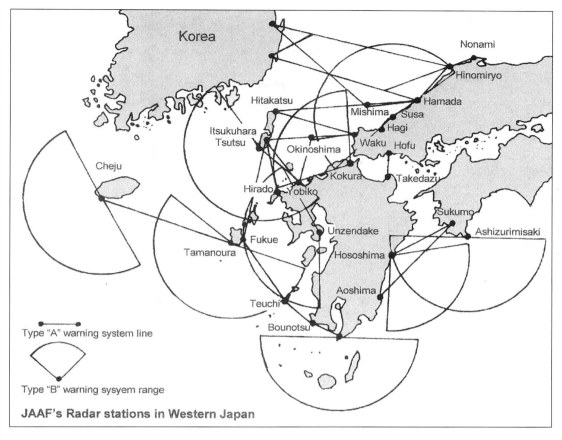

Type "A" warning system line

Type "B" warning sysem range

JAAF's Radar stations in Western Japan

The 51st Sentai was equipped with the Nakajima Ki-84 *Hayate* ('Frank') fighter at its base at Hofu airfield, Honshu. It was a relatively new unit, set up in April 1944 at the same time as the 52nd Sentai, which was also equipped with the 'Frank'. The 59th from Ashiya – proud veterans of the Khalkin Gol Incident in May 1939 (when the Soviet Union and Japan clashed over the disputed border between Manchuria and Outer Mongolia), as well as the China War and the CBI – sported the sleek Kawasaki Ki-61 *Hien* ('Tony').

Together, these four army air groups had 89 fighters with which to tackle the B-29s. In addition, the Japanese Navy's 352nd and Omura Kokutais (air groups) also scrambled their fighters.

The Superfortresses, now 67 strong, were flying in threes and fours, and arrived over Yawata at between 20,000 and 26,000 ft. They were greeted by intense anti-aircraft fire. The honour of dropping the first bomb was given to Maj Donald J Humphrey's *POSTVILLE EXPRESS* (42-6279). Aboard the aircraft was Brig Gen Saunders and several war correspondents and photographers.

'Betty! Betty! Betty!' shouted the radioman, signalling to base that bombs were dropping on Japan. Other aircraft began dropping their loads too. Anti-aircraft guns dotted the sky with puffs of smoke, and *Ready Teddy* (42-6408) from the 468th fell, while eight others were damaged. After running through the gauntlet of flak, at 1632 hrs the Americans were faced with enemy fighters coming at them with a vengeance.

Japanese radar stations proved effective in detecting the advance of B-29s towards western Japan. A network of ground observation posts in China also sent information of B-29 movements prior to the aircraft clearing the coast

13

Although bomber gunners reported some 50 fighters, there were actually more than double this number.

Col Robert Clinkscales of the 468th was leading his four-aircraft diamond formation in *Gertrude C* (42-6334), which was named after his mother. On the opening day of the war, Clinkscales had been co-pilot of the famed B-17 *The Swoose*. He later became Gen Douglas MacArthur's personal pilot, ferrying him around in an ex-Royal Australian Air Force DC-2. When the 58th BW was formed, he was one of the combat veterans selected for a leadership position. On this particular mission he had taken someone special along for the ride – with him in the cockpit was 'Sally', his cocker spaniel.

The 4th Sentai's 1Lt Isamu Kashiide, and his subordinate Sgt Shigeo Nobe, approached the large bomber formations in a head-on run. As Kashiide lined up an opponent with his 37 mm gun, Nobe, who was flying to his right, took a spontaneous decision and radioed that he was going to ram. Also in the aircraft was the rear-seat gunner, Sgt Denzo Takagi.

'Don't be hasty!' yelled Kashiide. But it was too late. Nobe was going to bring down his enemy at any cost. *Gertrude C* had just released its bombs

The 7.5 cm Type 88 anti-aircraft gun had a range of about 9000 m, although it was not accurate at such distances. Indeed, it was usually a lucky hit that brought down a B-29

Four pilots of the 468th BG who flew on the mission to Yawata on 20 August 1944. They are, from left to right, Col James V Edmundson, Col Robert Clinkscales, holding 'Sally', and Majs Don Humphrey and James Van Horn (*Don Humphrey*)

Pilots of the 4th Sentai are briefed at Ozuki in the spring of 1944. Sitting in the foreground, from left to right, are Sgt Minoru Uchida, 1Lt Isamu Kashiide and Sgt Shigeo Nobe. All three of these pilots would achieve multiple scores against the B-29 (*via H Sakaida*)

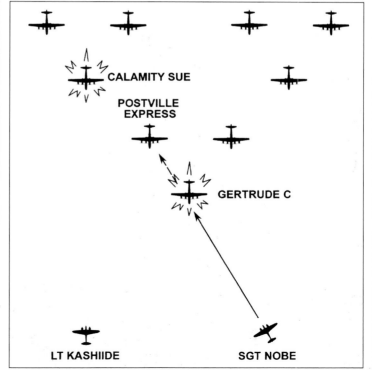

This diagram shows the collision course of Sgt Shigeo Nobe with Col Robert Clinkscales' *Gertrude C.* A tight formation contributed to the loss of two B-29s in the ramming attack

15

when Nobe manoeuvred his 'Nick' right into its flight path. He banked the aircraft to the right so that his right wing came vertical to Clinkscales' aircraft like an upraised knife. Pilots watched in horror as the 'Nick's' right wing sliced into the B-29's left wing between the tip and the No 1 engine. The bomber's wing tank exploded in a fireball, while the remains of Nobe's fighter cartwheeled backwards through the formation.

Maj Humphrey was flying behind Clinkscales' aircraft. Flaming debris flew over his right wing, nearly hitting him. Capt Ornell Stauffer, pilot of *Calamity Sue* (42-6368) in the trail position, was not so lucky. He pulled up sharply to avoid the wreckage, but his horizontal stabiliser was sheared off and the aircraft spun all the way down. The only person to survive the ramming and subsequent collision was Sgt Charles Shott, who parachuted down and was captured. He lived to return home.

The B-29s completed their mission with claims of 17 enemy aircraft shot down, 13 probables, and 12 damaged. On the debit side, 14 B-29s were lost, with eight damaged by flak.

The crew of the 794th BS's *POSTVILLE EXPRESS* (42-6279). Maj Don Humphrey pulled this aircraft up to avoid the wreckage of Sgt Shigeo Nobe's 'Nick', which had just rammed *Gertrude C* (*Don Humphrey*)

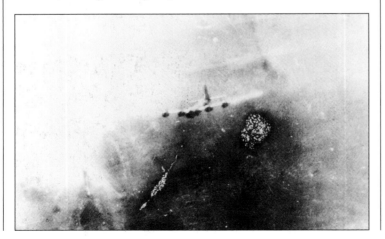

Impact! Sgt Shigeo Nobe rams his twin-engined fighter into *Gertrude C* on the left. This photograph was developed from a camera found in the wreckage of *Calamity Sue*

This photograph of *POSTVILLE EXPRESS* was snapped by an unknown crewman aboard the ill-fated *Calamity Sue* en route to Yawata

This second raid on Yawata was slightly better than the first. Two coke ovens were destroyed as 96 tons of bombs were dropped during the daylight attack. That night ten more B-29s attacked the same target, delivering 15 tons of bombs – all of them returned safely to base.

The Japanese claims for kills during the daylight raid would have been impressive if true. The 4th Sentai alone claimed an incredible 17 victories (eight unconfirmed) and another 17 damaged. Their high 'scorer' was M/Sgt Tatsuo Morimoto, who claimed three destroyed and four damaged, and won a personal citation for valour. Capt Masaji Kobayashi claimed two B-29s shot down, but he was hit and forced to make an emergency landing. Capt Toshio Sassa also believed that he had brought down a Superfortress, although his fighter had in turn been struck by defensive fire and he had parachuted to safety off Tsushima Island.

The 51st Sentai had put up 18 fighters and claimed two B-29s damaged, and the 52nd Sentai's 15 fighters claimed one Superfortress destroyed

The remains of a B-29 which was brought down on 20 August 1944 during the Yawata bombing raid

This Japanese newspaper photograph shows a B-29, hit by flak, falling to earth during the Yawata mission

jointly with the 59th north of Fukuoka. Even the 41-year-old CO of the 16th Air Brigade got into the action. Flying alone, Lt Col Tsuneemon Shindo claimed a B-29 over Yawata. Finally, the 59th Sentai believed it shot down one, with three unconfirmed and one damaged. In return, the unit lost one pilot, and had three Ki-61s seriously damaged.

RAID OVER MUKDEN

On 7 December 1944, XX Bomber Command sortied 108 Superfortresses on Mission 19 to destroy Japanese aircraft factories at Mukden, in Manchuria. But the raid was intended to accomplish more than that. It was meant as a morale-booster for more than 1600 Allied prisoners of war incarcerated there. For them, the raid would bring hope that the war could soon be over.

The bitterly cold Manchurian winter caused havoc for the bomber crews, for although the weather was crystal clear, the cold frosted the windows and reduced their ability to see their targets. 1Lt Tom Young, piloting *Mammy Yokum* (42-63536) of the 468th BG, recalled;

'Heading for the target, our nose section began to ice up inside, making it difficult to fly formation. Remembering what to do from the old days when my '29 Ford Coupe windows frosted up inside on a cold day before the engine warmed up, I asked my crew to go on oxygen, depressurised the

plane, and opened my side window. The gushing wind was extremely cold, but we had a much clearer view of what was happening around us.'

Ninety-one aircraft finally made it to the target area. Fighters from the 104th Sentai, the 25th and 81st Dokuritsu Chutai (independent squadron) and the Manchurian Air Force were there to greet them. Although bomber crewmen reported 185 single and co-ordinated attacks by 85 fighters, the actual number of attacking aircraft was considerably less.

Although ten bombers dropped their load on a railway yard well before they reached the primary target. 80 crews kept hold of theirs until they were over the target, then dropped their bombs despite a heavy smoke screen below.

One of the first B-29s lost during the raid was *GALLOPIN GOOSE* (42-6390) of the 468th BG, piloted by Capt Roger Parrish. About 15 minutes from the target, Sgt Shinobu Ikeda of the 25th Dokuritsu Chutai, flying a 'Nick', made a tail run against *Windy City II* (42-24486). The bomber gunners hit the right engine of the twin-engined interceptor and set it on fire. They also shattered the canopy.

Ikeda dived down, regained control of his fighter, and intentionally rammed the tail section of *GALLOPIN GOOSE* – this was the first recorded ramming over Manchuria. The stricken B-29 went straight down, and only one parachute was seen. The lone survivor was S/Sgt Arnold G Pope, who later said, 'I suppose all crew members other than myself are dead. I saw no other 'chutes emerge from the plane'. Sgt Ikeda died when his Ki-45 crashed.

The Japanese were determined to make the Americans pay a heavy price, and *"humpin honey"* (42-6299) of the 462nd BG was rammed by a Nakajima Ki-44 'Tojo' piloted by either Sgts Tadanori Nagata or Yoshihiro Akeno from the 104th Sentai – both men were killed in action.

'The ship either exploded or busted in the blister section, throwing the left gunner and myself clear of the plane', recounted S/Sgt Walter Huss,

GALLOPIN GOOSE of the 794th BS/468th BG was rammed in the tail section by Sgt Shinobu Ikeda in a 'Nick' during the 7 December 1944 mission to Mukden, in Manchuria

The shattered remains of *GALLOPIN GOOSE* lie in a field outside Mukden. Only a single crewman from the B-29 succeeded in bailing out prior to the aircraft hitting the ground

"humpin honey" of the 770th BS/462nd BG was also rammed over Mukden, falling victim to a 'Tojo' fighter of the 104th Sentai. Only two crewmen parachuted and survived as PoWs

The original crew of *"humpin honey"*. Standing, from left to right, are 1Lt Aurelius Colby (pilot), Harmony, Payne, Brewer, and Brown. Bottom, again from left to right, are Lawhon, Brown, Kirby, Blevins and Sgt Walter Huss. The crew had drastically changed by the time this machine was lost on the Mukden mission, with only Colby and Huss still remaining (*Walt Huss*)

one of two survivors. 'Neither one of us knows how we got out of the ship, so the only explanation we have is that the ship either exploded or busted in the blister section, which is the central fire control room, throwing the two of us clear of the plane'.

Both S/Sgt Huss and T/Sgt Ken Beckwith had to endure a court-martial by a Japanese military 'kangaroo' court on charges of bombing civilian targets. They were convicted, and sentenced to four months in solitary confinement. After ten months of hell, they were liberated by Russian troops at the end of the war.

2Lt Fumiro Sou attempted to ram *Georgia Peach*, but the nose gunner 'flamed' him. His 'Oscar' clipped the bomber's propeller and Sou was thrown out of his blazing fighter. In the confusion of combat, the pilot believed that he had destroyed the bomber, and was duly awarded the Bukosho for his daring feat. A rare cloth Bukosho is sewn on to his uniform (*K Osuo*)

The camel markings seen on this crumpled pile of wreckage indicate that B-29 42-6262 *Round Trip Ticket* had flown supply missions over the Himalayan Mountains prior to becoming a bomber proper with the 444th BG

Meanwhile, from the ground, Allied prisoners watched with intense fascination as the B-29 formation flew overhead and Japanese fighters made their runs. Roy Weaver recalled 'watching the Nip fighter dive right into one B-29, and seeing the exploding aftermath of the hit, the pieces falling from the sky. Awesome is the only word I can think of – a deadly awesome'.

Maj Douglas Hatfield, in *Georgia Peach* (42-63356) of the 468th, would count his blessings. 2Lt Fumiro Sou, an instructor in the 4th Training Squadron, had his sights on Hatfield's aircraft. He got to within 300 yards of the Superfortress when the American nose gunner hit his 'Oscar's' engine and set it on fire. The fighter banked to the right, clipped the bomber's No 1 propeller, then cartwheeled over the left wing, throwing the pilot out. Sou parachuted to safety and claimed to have brought down the B-29. For his daring, he received the Bukosho (B Class). However, in February 1945, he was to perish in a training accident. *Georgia Peach* returned safely to base with a damaged prop.

Another victim of a Japanese fighter was *Round Trip Ticket* (42-6262) from the 444th BG, piloted by Maj Carl R Barnes. Crewman T/Sgt Paul S Salk remembers;

'It was in the back of plane '584 and on the right side. I later noticed that '262 had dropped back and then disappeared. It had bombed the target with the formation. I then saw a "Nick" make a pass on '262 after bombs away.'

Mission 19 cost XX Bomber Command seven B-29s. Four were either shot down or rammed and three were operational losses. The Japanese lost five pilots and six aircraft – two 'Tojos', an 'Oscar', a 'Nick' and a fixed-landing gear Type 97 'Nate' from the Manchurian Air Force. The 'Nate', piloted by 2Lt Sono-o Kasuga, reportedly rammed a B-29 and he was killed. In all, the units claimed a total of 15 B-29s destroyed!

There would be only one more bombing raid on Manchuria before the 58th BW turned its attention to other targets in the CBI. On 21 December 1944, Mukden was raided by 40 Superfortresses, which dropped 88 tons of

'Diamond 33' on the fin identifies this B-29 as a 444th BG aircraft, and '6262' confirms that it was *Round Trip Ticket* from the 6th BS. It was most likely shot down by a 'Nick'

A Japanese soldier holds up a flak jacket found in the wreckage of *Round Trip Ticket* . . .

. . . and an oxygen mask

***Round Trip Ticket* again. A life raft was standard survival equipment aboard all B-29s**

Manchurian Air Force pilot 1Lt Sono-o Kasuga was killed in a ramming attack while flying a fixed-landing gear 'Nate'. This pre-war fighter aircraft was considered obsolete by the start of the Pacific War, being armed with just two 7.7 mm machine guns

bombs with little result. The Japanese defenders were all over the bombers, and B-29 42-24715 of the 468th BG, piloted by Capt Charles Benedict, was rammed by 2Lt Tahei Matsumoto, flying for the Manchurian Air Force – there were no survivors. The B-29's bombardier, Lt Dailey, and the navigator, Lt Evans, had married twin sisters, both of whom had babies in the summer of 1944.

Matsumoto's colleague, 2Lt Naruo Nishihara, apparently tried to ram another aircraft and was shot down, while Capt John Campbell's *Wild-Hair* (42-24505) from the 462nd was knocked out of the sky by a burst bomb. These were the only two B-29 losses on this mission.

By the end of March 1945, XX Bomber Command had ceased operations in the CBI. The 58th BW was transferred to the Marianas to join XXI Bomber Command, where it would carry on the campaign against the Japanese homeland.

JAAF VERSUS THE 73rd BW

Brig Gen Haywood Hansell flew the first B-29 (*Joltin' Josie*, 42-24614) into Saipan on 12 October 1944. As commanding officer of Superfortress operations in the CBI, Hansell was a consummate B-29 man, with a wealth of experience. He was also the author of the influential document *AAF Air War Plan APW-42* (the Strategic Bombing Campaign against Germany and Japan).

When the new Twentieth Air Force was formed in April 1944, Gen Henry 'Hap' Arnold was given the job of leading it. 'Possum' Hansell was

Brig Gen Haywood 'Possum' Hansell, the first CO of XXI Bomber Command (*Josh Curtis*)

Capt Ralph Steakley's F-13 was the first B-29 to be seen over Tokyo, and after the mission the crew named their aircraft *TOKYO ROSE*. In this publicity photograph taken for the newspapers back home, Capt Steakley is seen on the far right (*John Mitchell*)

selected both as his chief of staff and commander of XXI Bomber Command. His assignment was to start the bombing destruction of Japan from bases in the Marianas.

On 30 October, the first two photo-reconnaissance F-13 Superfortresses arrived on Saipan. Two days later, Capt Ralph Steakley was given the honour of piloting the first American aircraft over Tokyo since the 'Doolittle Raiders' back in April 1942. When the citizens of Tokyo looked up high into the sky on the afternoon of 1 November 1944, they were met with an unusual sight. They had never seen an aircraft flying so high over their city.

What they were gazing at was lone F-13 42-93852 of the 3rd Photo Group, cruising leisurely over the Kanto (Tokyo) plains at 32,000 ft, snapping photographs. The crew could see the hustle and bustle of a major metropolitan city on a lazy afternoon, and they paid particular attention to the heavy industrial areas concentrated along the shore from Tokyo to Yokohama.

The Japanese public was unaware of the impending devastation this lone aircraft would bring, but the solitary intrusion did cause a great deal of consternation among them. The Army's 47th Sentai, which had earned battle honours over Singapore and Burma in 1942, was on duty that day, and scrambled every available fighter from its base at Narimasu airfield.

The 47th was equipped with the Nakajima Ki-44 *Shoki* ('Tojo'). A rugged combat interceptor noted for its fast climb, it could reaching 5000 m (16,405 ft) in four minutes and seventeen seconds. The 'Tojo' was

Pilots of the 2nd Chutai/47th Sentai are seen on New Year's Day 1944 at Narimasu airfield, Tokyo. Note the 40 mm cannon fitted in the wing of the 'Tojo' fighter behind them (*K Osuo*)

armed with four 12.7 mm machine guns (a pair mounted in the nose and one gun in each wing), its service ceiling was rated at 11,200 m (36,745 ft), and it had a maximum speed of 605 kmh at 5200 m (376 mph at 17,060 ft). Japanese pilots would frequently mistake the aircraft for the appreciably larger American P-47 Thunderbolt.

As they began their pursuit at 1300 hrs, the pilots of the 47th knew the circumstances were hardly ideal. They were flying fully-fuelled and armed aircraft, which badly affected the climbing performance of the Ki-44. Furthermore, the 'Tojo' had not been designed for high-altitude flying. Indeed, at its highest ceiling, the fighter literally only 'floated' in the sky, and instantly dropped hundreds of metres if a turn was made.

With a lower wing load, the Army's Type 1 *Hayabusa* ('Oscar') and the Navy's standard A6M Zero fighter were better at manoeuvring at such high altitude. However, a great deal was expected of the 'Tojo' – in the fight against the B-29s, high speed and a good rate of climb were needed to catch the Americans, and that is what the Ki-44 could provide.

The 1st Chutai (squadron) doggedly pursued the F-13 as the 2nd and 3rd Chutais followed. Capt Jun Shimizu, who was in the lead, could see the four-engined behemoth sailing away, as he and his men were hard pressed to reach 9000 m – a few actually climbed 500 m higher. Capt Shimizu and 1Lt Shinichi Matsuzaki were completely frustrated. Two formations of the 1st Chutai pointed their noses up at the intruder about 1000 m above them and, with almost no control, fired short bursts.

Capt Steakley and his F-13 crew probably did not even realise they were being fired upon. They returned to Saipan, and that night photo-analysts, excited and smiling, swarmed over fresh black and white prints taken on

Capt Jun Shimizu, leading the 1st Chutai of the 47th Sentai, fired on Steakley's F-13 in frustration high over Tokyo. Shimizu commanded the 1st Chutai from July 1944 until the end of the war

the mission. Crowded airfields, factories, refineries and shipping ports were clearly visible.

For their efforts, Capt Steakley was awarded the Distinguished Flying Cross and his men received the Air Medal. Their aircraft was given the name *TOKYO ROSE,* and it and the crew received huge publicity in newspapers back in the US. With a big fanfare, the 73rd BW was about to go into serious business.

Prior to attacks on the Japanese mainland actually taking place, efforts were made to thwart the construction of the huge airfields on Saipan. In the first bombing attack there, on the night of 2 November, ten Japanese Navy 'Betty' bombers of Attack Hikotai 703 sortied from Iwo Jima. Just after 0130 hrs Saipan time, the air raid alert was sounded. Only five bombs landed on Isley Field. 1Lt Francis Eaton and radar operator 2Lt James Ketchum, flying in a P-61 Black Widow of the 6th Nightfighter Squadron, brought down one of the intruders west of Saipan – in total, the Japanese lost three bombers on the mission.

Maj Robert K Morgan (left) and Brig Gen 'Rosie' O'Donnell engage in a last-minute discussion before entering *Dauntless Dotty*. This was the lead aircraft on the first Tokyo raid, on 24 November 1944. O'Donnell was CO of the 73rd BW (*Josh Curtis*)

At 0130 hrs on 7 November the Japanese came back, five of seven 'Bettys' launched making it to Saipan, but no bombs hit worthwhile targets. Their escort fighters strafed the runway on this occasion, but inflicted very little damage. They all escaped through the cloak of darkness.

FIRST STRIKE ON TOKYO

From the moment the intelligence officers got their hands on the reconnaissance photographs of the Tokyo area, Saipan was a flurry of

activity. The Musashino aircraft engine factory, which produced Nakajima units for fighters, was designated as primary target No 357. The docks were marked as secondary targets.

On 7 November Brig Gen Hansell sent an F-13 back to Tokyo to gather more information. The Japanese knew that 'snoopers' would be returning, so all Army and Navy air groups in the area were placed on stand-by. When the F-13 arrived, it was chased by more than 100 fighters, but at 32,000 ft it was beyond their reach. It went about its business and returned to Saipan with valuable aerial photographs.

Three days later the 497th BG's Capt John Garvin, in *Skyscrapper* (42-24599), flew over Tokyo acting as flak 'bait' to test the accuracy of the enemy's guns. His safe return spoke volumes. Mission No 7 was scheduled for the following day, but had to be delayed because of bad weather.

The first appearance of B-29s over Tokyo had so alarmed the Japanese that Maj Gen Kihachiro Yoshida, commander of the JAAF's 10th Fighter Division, ordered the air groups under his command to form air-to-air ramming sections. Each unit commander was to choose four pilots for this dangerous assignment. To reach the enemy flying at high altitudes, all armaments, armour plating and unnecessary equipment was removed from the fighters. It was discovered that by stripping out 200 kg of weight, the aircraft could climb between 500 and 1000 m higher.

The weather finally cleared on 24 November. At 0615 hrs, groundcrew and troops lined the runway to cheer as Superfortress *Dauntless Dotty* (42-24592) of the 497th BG took to the air to lead an armada of 111 B-29s. At the controls of the silver bird, which was loaded with two-and-a-half tons of GPs and incendiaries, was Brig Gen Emmett 'Rosie' O'Donnell, CO of the 73rd BW.

This diagram reveals just how extensive the radar coverage dotted along the southern Japanese coast was in 1944-45

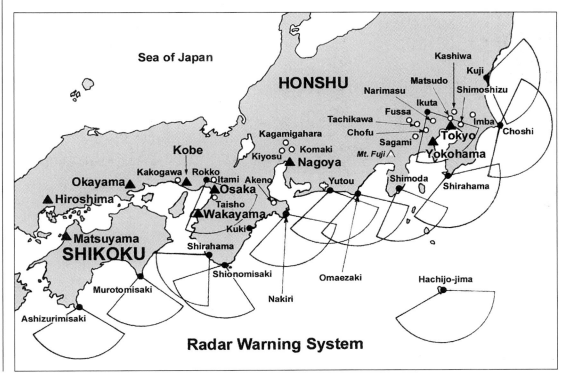

Scramble! Pilots of the 47th Sentai rush to their 'Tojo' fighters to effect an interception against 73rd BW B-29s on 24 November 1944 (*K Osuo*)

The 40 mm Ho-301 cannon was installed in only a handful of Ki-44-IIc 'Tojo' fighters for use against B-29s. Its unique self-propelled ammunition has 12 exhaust ports, and carried a high-explosive charge. The 40 mm round had an effective range of only 150 m, forcing the pilot to come within point-blank range of the B-29's defensive guns

Back in Tokyo, fighters given the task of ramming intruders were waiting. These aircraft were serving with the 47th Sentai at Narimasu airfield, the 23rd at Imba and the 70th at Kashiwa. All were equipped with 'Tojos'.

The American swarm, spearheaded by F-13s, made its way to Japan. The early-warning network, which consisted of radar stations on the islands of Ogasawara, in the Bonins, and Hachijojima, quickly notified the 10th Fighter Division. It in turn alerted the various air groups assigned to defend certain areas. It took roughly 85 minutes from the moment the intruders were detected by radar to position interceptors at high altitude.

As they waited for their first contact with the incoming Superfortresses, the Japanese pilots were having a hard time. Some were unable to maintain altitude, formation, or even stay in the zones they had been assigned. Their biggest problem was the surprisingly powerful jet stream of the prevailing

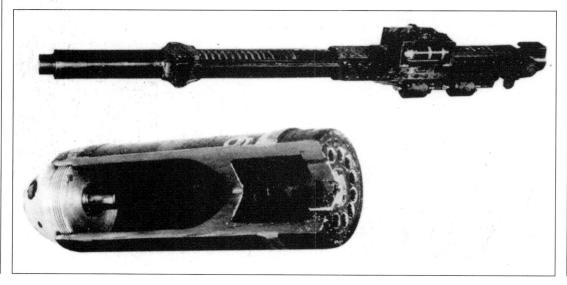

westerlies at high altitude, which would also hamper the B-29s. If their nose were put to leeward, the fighters would be swept away. The temperature was below -50°C.

However, not everything was stacked against the defending pilots. The chances for attacking the B-29s was increased because the massed formations flew on a fixed course, and aircraft were held steady during bombing runs. Their approach was usually detected far in advance by early-warning radar, which allowed the Japanese fighter pilots time to climb and wait.

What also helped the Japanese was when the American bombers flew independently to the 'rally' point. When almost at the coast, they would circle to reach bombing height, and continue circling while the formation leader shot off flares to get the aircraft into combat boxes.

By the time the B-29s arrived over their target, 17 bombers had aborted. The jet stream reached more than 130 mph and the target was clouded over. Only 27 bombed the Musashino plant from 27,000 ft, while 59 attacked the secondary targets. Six did not bomb at all due to mechanical problems. The engine factory sustained moderate damage, but certainly not enough to curtail production, and post-mission evaluation revealed that only about one per cent of the factory buildings had been destroyed.

Meanwhile, Maj Noboru Okuda, commander of the 47th Sentai, had tried to go 'big-game' hunting with a pair of 40 mm Ho-301 cannons. They were unusual weapons, with ammunition that did not use cartridges but a self-propelled explosive projectile much like a miniature rocket. The rate of fire was 450 rpm, but with a very short range of accuracy of just

1Lt Sam P Wagner and crew of the 870th BS/497th BG – Wagner is in the middle, squatting by his dog. Their aircraft was rammed by Cpl Yoshio Mita on 24 November 1944 over Tokyo. The only survivor was M/Sgt William Nattrass, standing at the extreme left (*Nattrass via J Curtis*)

150 m (490 ft). And each gun carried only ten rounds! At an altitude of 9000 m, Okuda made a frontal attack from above, and believed he hit his target. However, the lumbering bomber continued on as if unscathed.

The first B-29 victim on the mission was 1Lt Sam Wagner's 42-24622 from the 497th BG. Wagner's 'A-26' was flying in an outside position in formation when a 'Tojo' came in with guns blazing. Cpl Yoshio Mita of the 47th Sentai went in for the kill, and all the 0.50-cals on the B-29 were effectively silenced.

Cpl Fred Lodovici was tail gunner in *Haley's Comet* (42-24616), and he and the upper turret gunner began firing on Mita at 800 yards. They hit the incoming fighter but could not stop him. Lodovici later reported;

'He came in to about 150 or 200 yards just about even with the tail of Ship #26, and at that time our right gunner opened fire also. He appeared to hover for awhile in mid-air, and then rolled over the tail, his right wing hitting the vertical stabiliser, and then he rose up in the air and slid onto the left elevator. Then they both went down.'

Cpl Mita had cut off the right stabiliser and elevator of his target. The fighter burst into a fireball and fell from the sky. About 20 miles from shore, the Superfortress went into a spin and crashed nose first upside down – there were no survivors. The only other combat casualty from this mission was B-29 42-24679 from the 499th BG, the aircraft losing fuel and being forced to ditch – all 12 crewmen were rescued.

The Japanese defenders lost five fighters, and nine more were damaged. There were two reported rammings – one by Mita, and another by 1Lt Motokuni Ise of the 17th Dokuritsu Chutai. Ise was said to have rammed his opponent over Hachijo Island in a Mitsubishi Ki-46 'Dinah',

A twin-engined Ki-46-III-B 'Dinah' of the 17th Dokuritsu Chutai and an 18th Sentai 'Tony' undergo a field trajectory test at Chofu airfield in September 1944 (*K Osuo*)

about 300 km from Tokyo. The day's action had provided the 244th Sentai with its first battle against the B-29, the unit claiming one bomber shot down and another damaged, for the loss of one pilot. The Navy's 302nd Kokutai, which was placed under the Army Defence GHQ, had achieved virtually nothing, however. The unit had sent up no less than 48 Mitsubishi J2M3 'Jacks', but had only managed to claim one B-29 damaged.

Maj Gen Yoshida was incensed by the 10th Fighter Division's embarrassing results, and ordered his air groups to double the number of ramming aircraft from four to eight.

STIRRING UP A HORNET'S NEST

Target 357, the Musashino factory, was the priority target for the Americans, and it had to be destroyed as quickly as possible. Brig Gen Hansell knew that by bombing Tokyo, he would stir up a hornet's nest, and he was proved right. On 27 November the Japanese retaliated.

Twelve Zeroes from the Navy's 252nd Kokutai staged out of Iwo Jima and flew towards Isley Field, a distance of about 600 nautical miles. They were accompanied by two Nakajima C6N 'Myrt' reconnaissance aircraft. The daring commando raid was led by Lt(jg) Kenji Omura. In the final leg of their journey, the 'Myrts' separated and the fighters dropped down until they were only five metres above the water. One Zero flew too low and damaged its propeller in a wave, and PO1/c Takeo Matsushita was forced to make an emergency landing on Pagan Island.

The remaining 11 Zeroes caught the Americans flat-footed when they appeared over Isley Field. They strafed and destroyed four B-29s, including *Skyscrapper*. In the middle of this attack, Brig Gen Hansell got into a Jeep and headed up to Isley Field. Horrified to see a Zero coming straight towards him, he stopped and took cover. The fighter passed overhead without firing a shot and landed on the airfield. Hansell then watched in amazement as the Japanese pilot climbed out and fought airfield personnel with his pistol until they killed him.

None of the Zero pilots returned from this mission, and most were shot down by anti-aircraft fire around the airfield. One pilot, Leading Airman Tetsu Meijo, made it to Pagan Island, where he was in a landing pattern with his wheels down when he was jumped by four P-47 Thunderbolts. 1Lt James A DeYonker of the 333rd Fighter Squadron (FS) brought him down in a coconut grove.

The Japanese attack reaffirmed Hansell's conviction that the 73rd BW was on the right track. Bad weather had been a thorn in his side, but he was determined to increase the pressure on the Japanese.

By the time the raid on Isley Field was mounted, the Japanese had been through several high-altitude combats against the B-29s over Tokyo. The defending pilots had became accustomed to flying in the thin air, and they knew what to expect from their opposition – the pilots also compared notes and traded experiences.

Several improvements were made to their fighters as well. For example, in the 47th Sentai the diameter of the Ki-44's lubricant pipe was enlarged so that more oil flowing around the engine would prevent it from losing power at high altitude. Meanwhile, engineers at Mitsubishi fitted wider 'paddle' propeller blades to the Navy's 'Jacks' to improve efficiency at altitude. Just this little change added an extra 1000 m to the service ceiling.

On 3 December 86 Superfortresses left Saipan for Tokyo, and once again their target was the engine factory. Beautiful Mt Fuji, snow-capped and looking like a picture postcard, provided a convenient landmark as it rose over the horizon.

In the cramped radio compartments, radiomen listed in on 'Radio Tokyo's' propaganda programme 'Humanity Calls', but not for entertainment purposes. They hoped to use their radio compass to ride the radio waves straight to Tokyo. However, the enemy was not so accommodating, and the programme abruptly left the air – a sure sign they had been alerted.

Capt Teruhiko Kobayashi would play a pivotal role in the defence of the Imperial capital. Appointed to lead the 244th Sentai, the charismatic 24-year-old had become the youngest air group commander in the JAAF. On arriving at his post, Capt Kobayashi had told his men, 'Commanding a fighter unit should be done in the air. Follow me!'

The 244th had an air-to-air ramming section which had been formed in October 1944 and named Shinten Seiku Tai. The tails of its 'Tony' aircraft were painted red, onto which the first syllable of the pilot's surname was added in white phonetic lettering. Its pilots went into combat fully armed.

On this December day, the air raid alert was issued at 1145 hrs and the ramming section took off an hour later. First in the air was 1Lt Toru Shinomiya, followed by Cpl Masao Itagaki, WO Gannoshin Sato and Cpl Matsumi Nakano. Knowing they would probably not return alive,

Beautiful Mt Fuji served as a natural landmark for the B-29 formations on their way towards Tokyo

Capt Teruhiko Kobayashi was promoted to CO of the 244th Sentai at just 24 years of age, thus becoming the youngest air group commander in the JAAF. The painted silhouettes of B-29s denote victories scored by pilots flying this particular Ki-61. The sixth kill came about due to a ramming attack by Kobayashi (*Maru*)

The *Asahi Shimbun* newspaper article made a hero of Cpl Matsumi Nakano of the 244th Sentai following his exploits on 3 December 1944 over Tokyo. His Ki-61 chewed off the tail of a B-29 flown by 1Lt Charles Fetter, and then he force-landed his fighter in a rice paddy. Thanks to the story's diagram, and poetic licence on the reporter's behalf, a myth was created in which Nakano supposedly rode the back of the B-29 like a horseman! (*Y Kumoi*)

each pilot shook hands with their groundcrews, and thanked them for their efforts.

Some senior officers in the 73rd BW had decided to take part in the raid, with dire consequences. Piloting the lead bomber, 42-24656 ('Z-1'), was Col Richard King, CO of the 500th BG. Col Byron Brugge, Deputy Chief of Staff for Operations of the 73rd BW HQ, went along as an observer. The regular pilot, Maj Robert Goldsworthy, was also on board.

Within minutes of 'Z-1' dropping its load, a thin trail of white smoke or vapour was seen coming out of the No 3 engine. As soon as the engine was feathered, they lost speed and fell behind the formation. Goldsworthy remembers;

'Bombs were dropped at approximately two o'clock in the afternoon. Immediately after leaving the target, we were attacked by enemy fighters. In the resulting action, my aeroplane had three engines shot out, control cables shot away, and all its electrical and communication systems completely destroyed. One wing was blazing, and we had a large fire in the front cabin of the aeroplane. As the ship was out of control, we started bailing out at about 28,000 ft.

35

1Lt Toru Shinomiya (left) and Cpl Masao Itagaki both rammed B-29s on 3 December 1944. Shinomiya returned in this fighter with a damaged wing and Itagaki parachuted. Both received the Bukosho for valour (*M Katoh*)

The Bukosho (Medal of Honour) citation issued to Cpl Masao Itagaki reads;

'The aforementioned pilot spotted 11 B-29s heading north-east from Narimasu at high altitude over the Imperial Capital when the enemy's main air force from the Marianas raided on 3 December 1944. He pursued them to Moriya Town, Ibaraki Prefecture, and approached a B-29 at the tail end of the formation. Cpl Itagaki dared to ram it, and inflicted such damage that it was observed to have been almost certainly downed. The pilot successfully survived by parachuting. Cpl Itagaki fully exhibited his fierce fighting spirit and excellent piloting skills in the action. His self-sacrificing service is a model for the fighter units, and he is hereby cited by the awarding of the Bukosho. Signed, Gen Keisuke Fujie, Commander of the East Army, 17 January 1945'

Japan's 'medal of honour' was the Bukosho, awarded in Class A and B. Most recipients were fighter pilots who scored successes against the B-29s, and almost all of them received the B Class, depicted here. It came in a balsa wood presentation box, and most often was accompanied by a citation scroll. The Bukosho was instituted through an Imperial edict by Emperor Hirohito on 7 December 1944. It broke with tradition in that it was conferred upon a living individual. Before this award, only the dead were officially recognised as heroes (*via H Sakaida*)

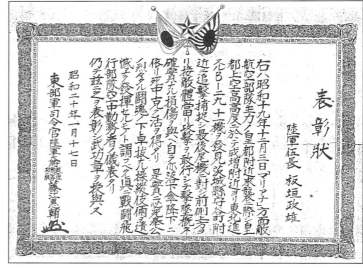

A part of the wreckage of B-29 42-24656, which had been carrying Cols Richard King and Byron Brugge, lies in a rice field at Jindai village, in Chiba prefecture (*Y Kumoi*)

'A fighter with red balls painted clearly on the fuselage made a head-on attack at us. It was firing at random, and passed right over our plane. The gunners opened fire and the fighter went down smoking and spinning.'

The fighter making the head-on run was flown by Capt Kobayashi. Despite the damage to his mount, he managed to get back to base and grab a replacement aircraft, but was too late to rejoin the fighting. Meanwhile, a dozen fighters had mauled Goldsworthy's B-29.

All but three of the American crew managed to bail out. 1Lt Walter J Patykule bailed out with his parachute on fire and was killed, and 1Lt Henry H Warde, S/Sgt Carl T Wells and Sgt John A Wright landed with serious wounds and were sent to Chiba army hospital, where all three died the following day. On 11 February, Sgt Tom Geoffery starved to death at the 1st temporary army hospital in Tokyo, while Col Brugge died later at the same hospital, driven insane by brutal interrogation. Only Maj Goldsworthy, Col King and Cpl Harold Schroeder survived captivity.

At Matsudo airfield, home base of the 53rd Sentai, 1Lt Masato Tsuru demonstrates how to attack a B-29 in a head-on run. Their twin-engined 'Nicks' were armed with a 37 mm cannon in the nose and a pair of obliquely-mounted 20 mm cannon behind the cockpit for nightfighter use (*K Osuo*)

The 244th's Toru Shinomiya is seen following his promotion to major. He was killed on 29 April 1945 during a *kamikaze* mission in the defence of Okinawa (*K Osuo*)

As 'Z-1' headed down, it was rammed over Matsudo, in Chiba Prefecture, by a 'Nick' flown by Sgt Masami Sawamoto of the 53rd Sentai. Sawamoto was killed in the encounter.

While most JAAF fighters concentrated on the destruction of 'Z-1' on 3 December, the four 'Tonys' of the 244th Sentai's ramming unit had meanwhile climbed to 10,000 m and commenced patrolling in single file. Suddenly, their radios crackled, 'Six ducks intruding over Odawara!' The B-29s were soon spotted 1000 m below. 1Lt Shinomiya went into a sharp dive, followed by his colleagues. Each pilot aimed for a spot ahead of their target by mentally calculating their speed, hoping to intersect at the critical time. Nakano's first pass was a failure;

'I pulled the control lever and went up slightly forward of the B-29, making a pass from above. But the enemy almost grazed the nose of my plane and flew away again. At the same time I met with prop-turbulence from the B-29, and my aircraft fell to an altitude of 7000 m. I lost sight of both friendly and enemy planes.

Cpl Matsumi Nakano won the Bukosho for his ramming attack of 3 December 1944. He became a rare double Bukosho recipient when he rammed another B-29 on 27 January. His total wartime score was three B-29s destroyed, one damaged and two F6Fs shot down (*K Osuo*)

'I climbed back to 10,000 m and continued patrolling. After a while I received a radio transmission that 12 B-29s were coming in, and I knew that this would be my last chance. I changed to my favourite tactic, which was to attack from above, ahead and off to the flank.

'The B-29s' altitude was 9000 m and the altimeter of my plane indicated 9500. I was in an absolutely favourable position, but the shape of the enemy formation was a bit different from the previous one. With four planes in the front line, three on the right side and four on the left side, thus making a fan shape, they encircled the remaining one at the centre. My target was the one at the centre, and I began an attack run. I came under violent gunfire, but I dashed forward, not caring. I thought, "I've done it!" But I missed!'

After failing twice in his ramming attacks, Nakano sped forward into another echelon from behind. He did not connect, instead diving under a B-29. Pulling up, he prop-scythed the B-29's vertical stabiliser. A few minutes later, the B-29 ('T-10', 42-24735) of the 498th BG, piloted by

1Lt Charles E Fetter Jr, fell out of formation with a pack of fighters all over it. Nakano crash-landed in a rice paddy in Ibaraki prefecture.

Cpl Masao Itagaki recalled his own harrowing experiences;

'We could see the AA shells burst above the Tokyo skies at 10,250 m. As we headed towards Mt Fuji, I was thinking, "Here they come, here they come!" My chest pounded with excitement and I looked up to find what I knew was there. From the vain attempts of the anti-aircraft gunners to reach their targets, I knew exactly where to look. Sure enough, there they were!'

Aboard *Long Distance* (42-24544), Lt Don Dufford of the 498th kept a steady course as the Americans entered their bombing run through flak. Finally it was 'bombs away!' Seven 500-lb demolition and three 500-lb incendiary bombs fell earthward. Over the interphone, radioman Sgt Don M Frensley heard constant reports of flak and incoming enemy fighters. The turret gunner above his station was hammering away on his 0.50s. 'Hank, one closing in at 11 o'clock level . . . get him!' screamed a comrade.

Cpl Itagaki was calculating the airspeed to lead his fire onto the rapidly closing target;

'I closed and pulled the trigger, but there was no response from my guns! I cursed my guns, reached down and tried desperately to clear them. When I lifted my eyes, looming directly in front of me was a giant B-29!'

The 'Tony' pilot yanked his stick back, but it was too late. Sgt Frensley felt the unnerving impact in his windowless compartment, followed by a tremendous vibration. Something had hit the aircraft hard. 'I can only remember that I thought it was the end. In my bewilderment I waited, hoping to hear a good word over the interphone,' recalled Frensley.

The red-tailed 'Tony' had swerved slightly as gunners pumped slugs into its nose. Itagaki had missed the bomber's fuselage by inches, and his left wing had sliced the No 3 engine in half. The 'Tony' cartwheeled

Long Distance of the 875th BS/498th BG. She was rammed over Tokyo by Cpl Masao Itagaki of the 244th Sentai but survived

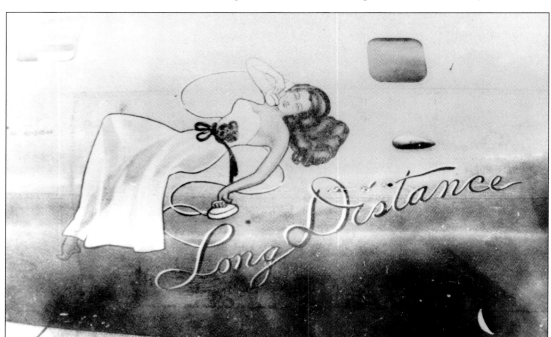

An article in the *Oklahoma City Times* shows the damage inflicted by Cpl Itagaki's ramming attack on *Long Distance*

Oklahomans Aboard Jap-Rammed B-29

Crew members of a B-29 based on Saipan Island examine an engine of their ship damaged when a Jap fighter plane tried to ram it on its return from a raid on Japan December 3. One is an Oklahoman, and the wife of another lives in Oklahoma City. Kneeling is Cpl. Joseph C. Cook, Tajunga, Calif., gunner. Standing, left to right: Lieut. Donald J. Dufford, Grand Junction, Colo., plane commander; Lieut. Drayton K. Finney, Miles, Ohio, navigator, whose wife lives at 709 NW 33; Cpl. George P. McGraw, Titusville, Pa., gunner; Sgt. Robert H. Jay, Hobson, Mont., gunner; Sgt. Don M. Frensley, Duncan, Okla., radio operator; Lieut. Roger S. Kolb, Spencer, Ind., flight engineer; Sgt. R. V. Rainer, Groesbeck, Texas, gunner, and Sgt. Salvatore A. Tartaglione, New York, central fire control gunner. (Wirephoto.)

towards the rear of the stricken bomber and cleared the rear gunner's compartment. Parts of the wreckage smashed into the right blister and caused sudden depressurisation, ripping the gunner's oxygen mask off his face. He fell forward and lost consciousness.

Itagaki was catapulted from his cockpit. 'My fighter smashed into the B-29 with such force, it popped open my parachute', he recalled. 'Then I spun around and around until I came down unharmed in a rice field'.

Back aboard *Long Distance*, the crew sprang into action. Radioman Sgt Salvatore Tartaglione rushed to save the right gunner. He revived him with his own oxygen mask as debris swirled around them. Suddenly, Tartaglione started to faint from lack of oxygen. The left gunner jumped in with his mask to save him. Meanwhile, the tail gunner and the central fire control operator kept the enemy fighters at a distance. The aptly named aircraft managed to go the full distance and return home.

The fighting spirit of the Shinten Seiku-Tai is reflected in Matsumi Nakano's post-war memoir;

'Tactics cannot be taught, and what was taught cannot necessarily lead to good results, but I think that tactics should be created by, and for, the pilot himself. The basis of my method was to attack an enemy plane by closing in with a fighting spirit, and to risk my life if necessary by being fully prepared to ram it in order to destroy it.

Cpl Matsumi Nakano's 'Tony' was exhibited at Mitsukoshi department store in Tokyo, this being the aircraft he was flying on 3 December 1944. The exploits of the 244th Sentai pilots in their battles against the B-29 received tremendous publicity (*S Hayashi*)

'There were not a few, however, who were intimidated by the tremendously powerful concentrated fire from a big formation of B-29s. They helplessly became the enemy's prey in the process of trying to evade it. We all have a strong tenacity for life, but I think that combat is a scramble for lives, and the one who confronts his rival by laying down his life becomes the victor.'

Returning to the 3 December battle, over Gotenba, north of Izu Peninsula, the 'Tojos' of the 70th Sentai were circling. In a pursuit, the prevailing westerlies would have pushed them eastward, so WO Ken-ichi

1Lt Toru Shinomiya's 'Tony' exhibited at Matsuya department store in the Ginza District of Tokyo – it was on public display until the end of January 1945. Note the fighter's damaged left wing (*S Hayashi*)

Hiratsuka, who had tangled with B-29s over Manchuria, judged that his opponents would descend after bombing, and he was right. He spotted a lone B-29 at 7000 m and made his move – a frontal diving attack. The Superfortress belched flames from the inside engine on the right wing and swerved to the left, but succeeded in leaving Hiratsuka far behind.

Elsewhere, the 47th Sentai's eight 'Tojos' attacked an eight-aircraft formation at about 9000 m over north-west Tokyo, making one pass after another. Two bombers streamed white smoke, but they would not go down. Capt Jun Shimizu, who had been one of the pilots to fire the opening shots against the 73rd BW back on 24 November, left his group to hunt on his own. He managed to damage one Superfortress, which left the scene trailing black smoke, but its gunners managed several hits in return.

Meanwhile, Lt Fetter's 'T-10', which had been damaged by Cpl Matsumi Nakano's ramming attack, was losing its battle to stay airborne and ran into more trouble. As Capt Toyohisa Komatsu of the 244th Sentai was peppering the wounded bomber over Tokyo Bay, Navy fighters crowded in. CPO Yoshio Nakamura, a veteran of the Rabaul battles in 1943, cruised in his 'Jack' at 10,000 m over the sea off Choshi. Flying into a strong headwind, he spotted a B-29 approaching some 1000 m below him. A frontal assault set the bomber on fire and the crew bailed out.

Another Navy comrade, CPO Takumi Sugitaki (a former *Shokaku* carrier pilot who also briefly fought at Rabaul), bounced a lone B-29 over the same area and cut the aircraft into three pieces with bursts from his 30 mm cannon. 'I saw gasoline flowing out of the B-29 like a geyser and it exploded', recalled the pilot. Some of the crewmen parachuted out. It is possible that the two Navy and one Army pilot had all delivered the *coup de grace* to the same B-29 – 'T-10'.

Mission No 10 had cost the 73rd BW five B-29s (four went down in the water) and the commander of the 500th BG. Bomber gunners claimed ten kills, but a further 13 B-29s were damaged. The Japanese 10th Fighter Division claimed the destruction of five B-29s (four by ramming) and lost six aircraft.

The Musashino engine factory had escaped destruction yet again.

22 DECEMBER 1944

Mission 14 was remembered for the mass confusion among formations of B-29s over Nagoya. The priority target on this raid was the Mitsubishi factory that produced aircraft engines. It was considered to be one of the two largest producers, supplying 40 per cent of all aircraft engines to nine airframe assembly plants throughout Japan. Seventy-eight aircraft took off for a daylight firebombing mission, with each aircraft loaded with two-and-three-quarter tons of M-76 petroleum gel-filled incendiary bombs.

About an hour out from the target, four 498th BG aircraft in a nine-strong formation dropped out because of mechanical problems and headed home. At about the same time the mission leader made two complete turns to allow a straggler to catch up, but through miscommunication with other crews his formation broke up. Once over the target, thick clouds forced the B-29s to bomb inaccurately by radar, and one formation dropped their load *40 miles* to the left of the factory.

Fighters from the 11th Fighter Division (16th Dokuritsu Chutai and the 56th Sentai) and Akeno Teaching Fighter Division were waiting for

A Ki-46-III-B 'Dinah' of the 16th Dokuritsu Chutai has its engines run up. Although one of the best JAAF high-altitude reconnaissance aircraft of the war, when armed with two 20 mm Ho-5 cannons in the nose, the 'Dinah' fared less well in its role as a B-29 interceptor due to its poor climbing speed (*K Osuo*)

the Americans. The radar reports passed on to Tokyo determined at an early stage that Nagoya was the intended target, so the 17th Dokuritsu Chutai and the 244th Sentai were also ordered to scramble. The latter unit, based at Chofu airfield outside Tokyo, sped 140 nautical miles south-west to greet the incoming Superfortresses over Atsumi peninsula. In the battle that followed, 'Tony' pilots claimed two B-29s shot down and one damaged.

Now it was the 56th Sentai's turn to get at the B-29s. A recent intercept mission had exposed drawbacks with their 'Tonys' at altitudes of more than 9000 m (29,500 ft) – bad oxygen feed, gun trouble and oil coagulation due to extreme cold. To give the fighter some advantage, it was decided to make it lighter, and two 20 mm cannon and some armour plating was removed.

'Good luck and happy hunting!' A 'Dinah' pilot of the 16th Dokuritsu Chutai receives a hearty send-off from colleagues before a sortie (*K Osuo*)

Tactically, air group commander Maj Haruyoshi Furukawa had also reached the conclusion that frontal attacks would be the only way of inflicting damage to the B-29s. His pilots duly prepared themselves for the possibility of ramming or collision.

There were so many enemy bombers coming into the Nagoya area from all directions that M/Sgt Tadao Sumi of the 56th Sentai was hard-pressed to defend the city. A former infantryman-turned pilot, he would nevertheless make a name for himself in the home defence operation. His flight, consisting of T/Sgt Shizusaku Mashimo and S/Sgts Koji Hidaka and Yukio Miyamoto, first made contact with the enemy at 1336 hrs on the east side of Nagoya as a formation of five B-29s came in at 9500 m. The four 'Tonys' attacked, forcing the formation to turn away after damaging one aircraft. Six minutes later they intercepted a further six Superfortresses, and reported one shot down.

Pilots of the 56th Sentai scramble towards their 'Tonys' at Itami airfield on 18 December 1944. On that day, the 73rd BW raided Nagoya and lost only one B-29 over the target, with two ditching and one crashing on return (*K Osuo*)

M/Sgt Tadao Sumi is seen in the cockpit of his 'Tony' while serving with the 244th Sentai (*K Osuo*)

M/Sgt Tadao Sumi wearing his newly awarded A Class Bukosho. A renowned B-29 specialist, he shot down five, damaged four, and also destroyed a P-51 during his career (*Y Izawa*)

Only 48 bombers dropped on the primary target using radar, and the results were dismal, while 14 others attacked secondary targets. The widely scattered formations withstood no fewer than 508 passes by Japanese fighters.

THE DRAGON LADY (42-63425) from the 497th BG, piloted by Capt Howard Clifford, was rammed over its target and the top portion of its tail shaved off. The aircraft somehow made it back to Saipan, however.

T/Sgt Kobayashi of the 17th Dokuritsu Chutai spotted a formation of B-29s coming in across Suruga Bay from the west, and he carefully manoeuvred his twin-engined Ki-46-IIIB 'Dinah' over an intended victim. Mentally calculating the speed of both his aircraft and the B-29, he pulled ahead and dropped a 50-kg phosphorous cluster bomb. The resulting explosion was spectacular, but the B-29 failed to drop, although its landing gear came down when the blast damaged either its electrical or hydraulic system. A B-29 with its wheels down provided 1Lt Mitsukuni Takahashi, sitting back in the observer's seat, with a photograph opportunity. The bomber turned to the south and flew off.

In total that day, the JAAF claimed 16 B-29s destroyed and another 25 damaged for the loss of four of their own. Three pilots were reported killed in ramming attacks, and Cpl Setsuo Koai of the 56th Sentai was shot

THE DRAGON LADY of the 871st BS/497th BG had its tail shaved off by a Japanese fighter, but its crew still managed to coax the bomber home. It subsequently survived the war

Capt Junichi Ogata points to a map to explain his movements to Maj Haruyoshi Furukawa, CO of the 56th Sentai. They had just returned from a night interception on 22 December 1944 over Nagoya. Leading B-29 hunter M/Sgt Tadao Sumi can be seen between Ogata and Furukawa (K Takaki)

down when he dashed into a ten-aeroplane formation of B-29s coming from the direction of Hamamatsu. B-29 gunners claimed nine shot down, 17 probables and five damaged.

The 73rd BW's 497th lost two B-29s when they were forced to ditch, *New Glory* (42-24756) coming down en route to the target, and 42-24733 while returning. None was lost over Japan. Another struggled back to base so badly damaged that it became a trainer, never flying in combat again.

Maj Furukawa gave his assessment of the 73rd BW attack on Nagoya;

'The B-29s' bombing was very exact and successful in spite of their release at high altitude. Black columns of smoke rose high into the sky and flames were seen spreading violently.'

47

27 DECEMBER 1944

By the end of 1944 the 73rd BW was still trying to knock out the seemingly untouchable Musashino engine factory. Mostly unscathed, it mocked and taunted Brig Gen Hansell. Mission 16, slated for 27 December, was the last daylight B-29 bombing mission to Japan of 1944, and it was another futile exercise.

Seventy-two Superfortresses took off from Saipan and lumbered their way towards Tokyo. One B-29 (42-24613) from the 498th lost two engines immediately after take-off and went down in the sea between Saipan and Tinian – only three of the crew survived. Thirty-nine aeroplanes bombed the primary target, but due to the tremendous jet stream, accuracy suffered and the engine plants were again spared.

The JAAF was waiting anxiously for the intruders with the 28th, 53rd, 70th and 244th Sentais. The Navy's 302nd Kokutai also sent up four Zeroes, eight Nakajima J1N1-S 'Irvings', six Yokosuka D4Y2 'Judy' nightfighters and one Yokosuka P1Y2 'Frances'. More than 272 fighter attacks would be recorded by the B-29 crews.

The most heroic episode of this mission (from both sides) involved the ramming attack against *UNCLE TOM'S CABIN NO.2* (42-24642) of the 498th BG. It was an aerial slaughter witnessed by thousands of Japanese over Tokyo and anguished B-29 crews who could not help. Maj John Krause, the squadron operations officer, was piloting *UNCLE TOM'S CABIN NO.2*, filling in for the regular aircraft commander who had been hurt the previous day in a jeep accident. As the lead aircraft of the third element in a nine-aircraft formation, it was one minute from bomb release when its troubles began.

Capt Nagao Shirai of the 244th Sentai led his three-aeroplane flight of 'Tonys' and attacked a nine-aircraft formation flying eastward over Otsuki, but without success. 1Lt Chuichi Ichikawa's three-aircraft flight also attacked this same formation and damaged two B-29s, one of which was *UNCLE TOM'S CABIN NO.2*. A 'Tony' sliced downward at a 45-degree angle, narrowly missing 1Lt Walt Sherrell's *Southern Belle* (42-63478).

UNCLE TOM'S CABIN NO.2 of the 874th BS/498th BG apparently sustained damage to its nose section at some stage, and this was subsequently repaired, hence the NO. 2 designation. It was rammed twice, and then overwhelmed by a horde of fighters on 27 December 1944 (Josh Curtis)

Sherrell pulled up and the 'Tony' flashed underneath. A split-second later, his tail gunner yelled, 'Oh my God! He rammed Major Krause!'

According to Japanese eyewitness accounts, MSgt Takeo Yoshida of the 244th Sentai rammed Krause's 'T-25' on the right side, knocking the No 3 engine off and making a large gash in the fuselage. The attack had not been frontal, instead coming from above and behind. Padding and debris blew out of the bomber as it suddenly depressurised. Yoshida's parachute failed to open, and his body fell on Nakano ward in Tokyo. He was probably dead anyway, killed by the impact with the bomber.

Because the B-29 formation was on the bombing run, the aircraft could not leave their position to cover their damaged colleague. Krause's aircraft was smoking heavily, and on its own – its gunners put up a tremendous fight as a horde of Japanese fighters tore into it. The Superfortress went into a spin, but recovered at 20,000 ft, flying below and parallel to the squadron. The Japanese fighters were determined to bring it down, and they made pass after pass. 2Lt Toshio Masuda of the 53rd Sentai chased it in his 'Nick' and pumped 200 rounds from his obliquely-mounted cannon into the belly of the bomber from 100 m below. The B-29 began losing altitude, trailing even more black smoke, and navy fighters took their turn, firing into the beast which would not die.

2Lt Yasuo Watanabe of the 53rd aimed his twin-engined 'Nick' at the flying wreck. Diving below the enemy formation, he accelerated, raised the nose and rammed it on the left inside engine. Watanabe was killed when his Ki-45 crashed in a ball of fire near a railway bridge on the Arakawa river.

UNCLE TOM'S CABIN NO.2 finally succumbed to overwhelming odds and went down into Tokyo Bay. Three (*text continues on page 64*)

Members of *Hagure-Tai*, a ramming division of the 244th Sentai, pose for a group shot in November 1944. These pilots are, from left to right, 1Lt Toru Shinomiya (leader), Cpl Masao Itagaki, M/Sgt Takeo Yoshida and Cpl Tadashi Abe (*I Shinomiya*)

COLOUR PLATES

1
Ki-44-II-Otsu of the 3rd Chutai/47th Sentai, Chofu airfield, October 1944

2
Ki-61-I-Hei of the 2nd Chutai/244th Sentai, flown by M/Sgt Tadao Sumi, Chofu airfield, November 1944

3
Ki-45-KAI of the 3rd Chutai/53rd Sentai, flown by Sgt Nobuji Negishi, Matsudo airfield, November 1944

4
Ki-44-II-Otsu of the 47th Sentai Shinten Seiku Tai, flown by M/Sgt Isamu Sakamoto, Narimasu airfield, late 1944

5
Ki-46-III-KAI of the 16th Independent Chutai, Taisho airfield, December 1944

6
Ki-46-III-KAI of the 17th Independent Chutai, Chofu airfield, December 1944

7
Ki-46-III-KAI of the 28th Sentai, flown by T/Sgt Etsuo Kitagawa, Togane airfield, December 1944

8
Ki-45-KAI-Ko of the 2nd Chutai/4th Sentai, flown by Lt Isamu Kashiide, Kozuki airfield, late 1944

9
Ki-61-I-Tei of the 244th Sentai *Shinten Seiku Tai*, flown by section leader Lt Tohru Shinomiya, Chofu airfield, December 1944

10
Ki-61-I-KAIc No 3024 of the 244th Sentai, flown by Group CO Capt Teruhiko Kobayashi, Chofu airfield, late January 1945

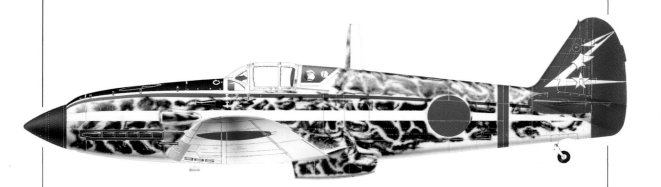

11
Ki-61-I-KAIc No 3295 of the 244th Sentai, flown by Group CO Capt Teruhiko Kobayashi, Chofu airfield, late January 1945

12
Ki-61-I-KAIc of HQ flight/244th Sentai, flown by T/Sgt Kiyoshi Ando, Chofu airfield, late January 1945

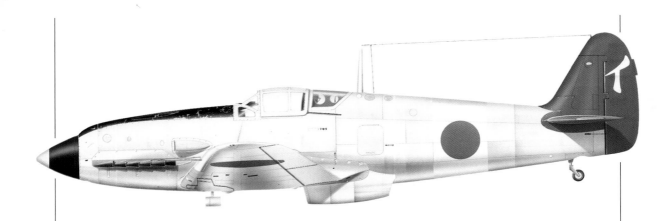

13
Ki-61-I-Hei of the 244th Sentai, flown by Sgt Masao Itagaki, Chofu airfield, January 1945

14
Ki-61-I-Hei of the 18th Sentai/6th Shinten Seiku Tai, flown by 1Lt Mitsuo Oyake, Kashiwa airfield, January 1945

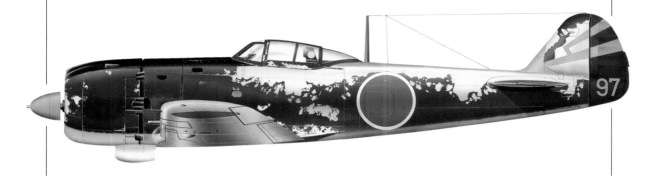

15
Ki-84-Ko of the 3rd Chutai/103rd Sentai, flown by 1Lt Shigeyasu Miyamoto, Itami airfield, January 1945

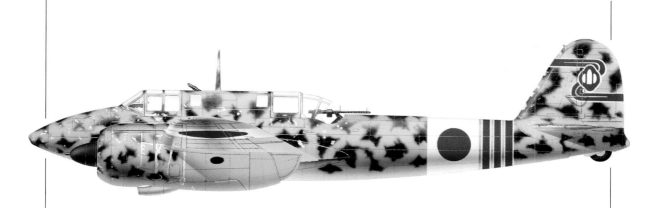

16
Ki-45-KAI of the 2nd Chutai/4th Sentai, flown by WO Sadamitsu Kimura, Kozuki airfield, January 1945

17
Ki-45-KAI of the 53rd Sentai Shinten Seiku Tai, Matsudo airfield, February 1945

18
Ki-84-Ko of the 51st Sentai, flown by Capt Tadao Ikeda, Shimodate airfield, February 1945

19
Ki-61-I-Hei of the 39th Educational Squadron, flown by M/Sgt Iwao Tabata, Yokoshiba airfield, March 1945

20
Ki-61-I-Tei of the 56th Sentai, Itami airfield, March 1945

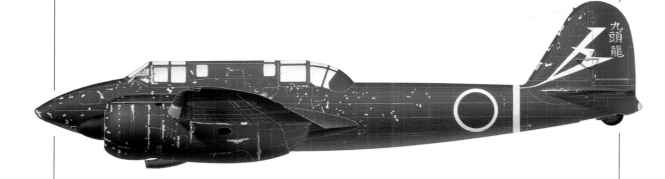

21
Ki-45-KAI-Ko of the 3rd Chutai/5th Sentai, flown by Chutai CO Capt Fujitaro Ito, Kiyosu airfield, March 1945

22
Ki-61-I-Tei of the 55th Sentai, Sano airfield, late March 1945

23
Ki-61-I-KAIc of the 244th Sentai, flown by Group CO Capt Teruhiko Kobayashi, Chofu airfield, April 1945

24
Ki-61-I-KAIc No 3024 of the 244th Sentai, flown by Group CO Capt Teruhiko Kobayashi, Chofu airfield, April 1945

25
Ki-45-KAI-Hei of the 4th Sentai/*Kaiten Tai*, flown by Lt Miosaburo Yamamoto, Kozuki airfield, April 1945

26
Ki-84-Ko of the Army Flight Test Centre, flown by M/Sgt Isamu Sasaki, Fussa airfield, May 1945

27
Ki-100-I of the 59th Sentai, Ashiya airfield, May 1945

28
Ki-100-I-Otsu of the 5th Sentai, Kiyosu airfield, June 1945

29
Ki-45-KAI of the 2nd Chutai/4th Sentai, flown by Lt Hannoshin Nishio, Kozuki airfield, June 1945

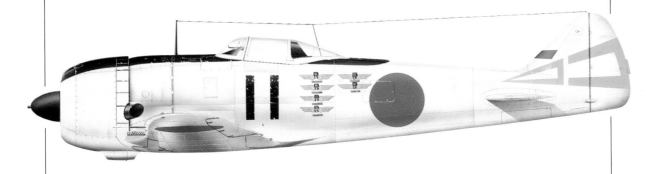

30
Ki-44-II-Hei of the 3rd Chutai/70th Sentai, flown by Capt Yoshio Yoshida, Kashiwa airfield, June 1945

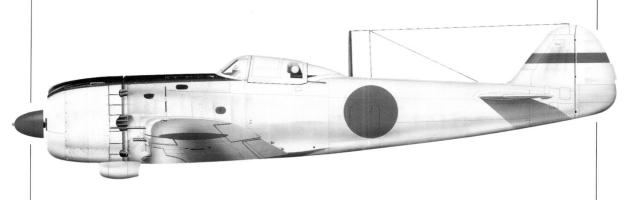

31
Ki-84-Ko of the 246th Sentai, flown by WO Kenji Fujimoto, Taisho airfield, July 1945

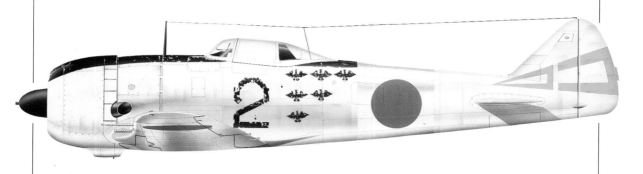

32
Ki-44-II-Hei of the 3rd Chutai/70th Sentai, flown by 2Lt Makoto Ogawa, Kashiwa airfield, June 1945

33
Ki-100-I-Ko of the 3rd Chutai/59th Sentai, flown by Chutai CO 1Lt Naoyuki Ogata, Ashiya airfield, August 1945

34
Ki-61-I-Tei of the 244th Sentai, Chofu airfield, August 1945

Tail Marking for Profile 1
Ki-44-II-Otsu of the 3rd Chutai/47th Sentai, Chofu airfield, October 1944. This marking is a stylised '47' for the 47th Sentai

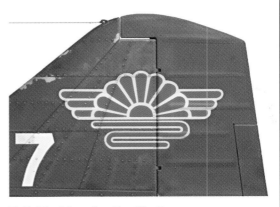

Tail Marking for Profile 5
Ki-46-III-KAI of the 16th Independent Chutai, Taisho airfield, December 1944

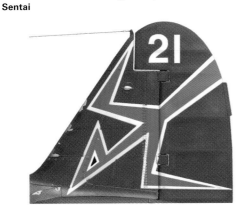

Tail Marking for Profile 19
Ki-61-I-Hei of the 39th Educational Squadron, flown by M/Sgt Iwao Tabata, Yokoshiba airfield, March 1945

Tail Marking for Profile 34
Ki-61-I-Tei of the 244th Sentai, Chofu airfield, August 1945

1

Blue silhouette of a B-29 with pointed wings and engines. This adorned a Ki-61 'Tony' of the 18th Sentai, flown by 2Lt Takeshi Nakamura. It denoted a shared victory claimed by the pilot, and this was the only kill marking to be painted behind the cockpit of this particular Ki-61

2

Red silhouette of a B-29. This marking was painted onto several of the Ki-61s flown by Capt Teruhiko Kobayashi of the 244th Sentai in 1944-45. Being CO of the unit, he frequently changed aircraft, taking his victory markings with him to his new fighter

3

Stylised shooting star, painted onto the Ki-61 'Tony' flown by Cpl Seiichi Suzuki of the 244th Sentai. He was shot down and killed (possibly in the fighter featuring this personal marking) on 16 February 1945. Suzuki was credited with destroying three B-29s and damaging a fourth

4

Black eagle with outspread wings and the titling 'B 29' beneath it. At least six of these kill markings were applied to WO Makoto Ogawa's well-weathered Ki-44 (of the 70th Sentai) during 1944-45, denoting his success with the 'Tojo' fighter

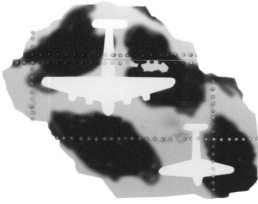

5

White kill silhouettes. More of Capt Kobayashi's victory markings, the fighter planform represents an F6F. Kobayashi did not down all of the aircraft represented by the markings on his Ki-61s! They actually denote kills claimed by all the pilots that flew this particular 'Tony'

6

White stylised eagle on a black background. This marking was used by 2Lt Miho Enda of the 55th Sentai, and it appeared on his Ki-61 'Tony'. It represented a victory he scored on 18 December 1944

7

Red stylised eagle with the titling '12.18' next to it. This victory marking appeared on a K-61 Tony of the 55th Sentai, the date '12.18' denoting a kill made on 18 December 1944. The aircraft's regular pilot was 2Lt Takeo Adachi, and it is unclear whether he made this particular kill – pilots did not have assigned aircraft, and they usually flew whichever machine was declared available at the time

9

Yellow stylised eagle's wings with 'B29' titling painted on them. This marking was used by the 70th Sentai's Capt Yoshio Yoshida to denote his kills, and it appeared six times on his Ki-44. Each featured an inscription in a red-outlined box, and this one reads, '20-4-13-Captain Yoshida' (the '20' is the Showa figure for the year 1945). The stylised wings were also used by legendary fighter ace Capt Tateo Kato to denote his victory markings during the China War. He painted the wings on his Ki-10 'Perry' whilst leading a squadron within the 64th Sentai

11

Small white Japanese flag. This victory marking was featured on a Ki-61 flown by 2Lt Shigeru Maeda of the 244th Sentai. This same type of victory marking was also used by Capt Tsutae Obara, again of the 244th – it is not known whether Obara was recording a fighter or a B-29 kill

8

Red B-29 silhouette with black Ki-61 'Tony' in profile across it. This kill marking represented Capt Teruhiko Kobayashi's ramming victory of 27 January 1945. This was the sixth victory credited to the aircraft, which was lost as a result of the collision

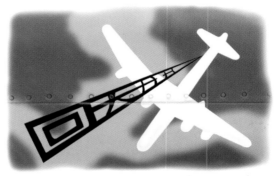

10

Silhouette of a white B-29 with its right wing tearing off. This was not a kill marking, but a unit marking of the Kaiten Tai, an air-to-air *kamikaze* ramming flight within the 4th Sentai. The Ki-45 that bore this particular marking was flown by 2Lt Miosaburo Yamamoto, who was killed over Fukuoka Prefecture on 18 April 1945 in a ramming attack. The *kanji* in the box reads 'Kaiten Tai'

12

Green shamrock on Ki-61 of Capt Kobayashi or Ishikawa

UNCLE TOM'S CABIN NO.2 in the moment of death, photographed heading down into Tokyo Bay. Only three men survived by parachuting

Billowing black smoke in Tokyo Bay marks the spot where *UNCLE TOM'S CABIN NO.2* hit the water

Fishermen retrieved a tyre and other floating debris from *UNCLE TOM'S CABIN NO.2*, along with three crewmen

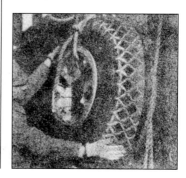

men managed to parachute into the water and were picked up by a fisherman – Maj William H Walker (Operations Officer of the 73rd BW HQ), 2Lt Stanley J Rebicki (bombardier) and Cpl Richard R Sandlin (tail gunner). All three were to survive Omori PoW Camp, but Maj Walker died from beri-beri aboard a hospital ship on 30 August – the day after he was liberated. A tyre, the tail and other parts from the bomber were fished out of the bay and exhibited in Hibiya Park in Tokyo from 1 to 20 February.

Bomber crewmen reported that Maj Krause's gunners downed at least nine enemy fighters, while his aircraft suffered three rammings. On both sides there were major errors in observation due to the heat of battle, the B-29 actually being rammed twice, not three times, and the gunners not downing nine or more enemy fighters. Krause was recommended for the Medal of Honor, but the father of one crewman complained that if Krause was worthy of this highest honour, then his son and the entire crew should also receive it. Maj Krause was initially awarded the Silver Star, which was subsequently upgraded to the second-highest American military decoration, the Distinguished Service Cross.

The third B-29 lost on the mission was *Heat's On* (42-24605), also from the 498th BG. Forced to ditch because of mechanical problems on its way back to base, only four crewmen were rescued – 1Lt Joseph M Gress (pilot) and 2Lts Robert L Lueckel (co-pilot), Ralph W Menkhus (navigator) and Warren L Hansen (flight engineer). They were picked up by the destroyer USS *Fanning* about 180 miles from Saipan at 2010 hrs on 28 December.

According to Japanese records, four fighters were lost flying against the B-29s, two due to ramming attacks. The JAAF claimed five B-29s shot

An exhibition at Hibiya Park in Tokyo in February 1945 featured Cpl Matsumi Nakano's 'Tony' and a mural depicting the inside compartments of a B-29. The nose wheel and auxiliary fuel tank from *UNCLE TOM'S CABIN NO.2* can be seen at the bottom and to the right in this photograph

down, five probables and 25 damaged. Japanese Navy pilots also made several claims, but they all appear to have been *Uncle Tom's Cabin*. The JNAF suffered no losses.

3 JANUARY 1945

The first bombing raid of 1945 was Mission 17, flown on 3 January. The 73rd BW still had not broken the back of the Musashino engine factory, despite repeated attempts, so taking a short break from target 357, the Twentieth Air Force ordered a test mission against Nagoya. Precision bombing had failed, and it was thought that torching the area might get better results. The production of many of the components used by the Japanese war machine was subcontracted to small family-run machine shops in residential areas, and hundreds of such businesses fed the main factory. If the factory could not be destroyed, then the machine shops around it could.

Each aircraft carried 14 M-69 incendiary cluster bombs designed to separate at 8000 ft into individual bombs. The goal was to scatter fire over a wide area, for Japanese houses were notoriously flammable because of their closely packed, all-wooden construction.

The mission started with 97 Superfortresses taking off. One aircraft, 42-24748 of the 498th BG, crashed for unknown reasons on Anatahan, a volcanic island in the Marianas, and the entire crew was killed. Along the way, a further 18 aircraft dropped out and returned to base.

The approach to the mainland was detected and the alarm went out to the 11th Fighter Division. Two 'Tony' units immediately took off to engage, the 55th Sentai scrambling from Komaki airfield and the 56th from its base at Itami, north of Osaka. In addition, the Navy's 210th

'Gertie' the bear, flanked by pilot Capt Hap Good on the left and radar operator Sgt Carl Vergin on the right. 'Gertie' was a Himalayan Sloth Bear cub raised by the crew. She went on three bombing missions to Japan in *Hap's Characters*, a 468th BG aircraft. Smuggled back to the US after the war, 'Gertie' eventually went to San Francisco Zoo, where she died in 1965 (*Tom Britton*)

Kokutai contributed 12 Zeroes, six 'Irvings' and nine 'Judy' nightfighters from its base at Meiji airfield, on the outskirts of Nagoya.

Fifty-seven bombers dropped their loads on the primary target while twenty-one hit secondary targets. Overall, the fire bombing was not very successful. Japanese fighters made 346 recorded passes.

Leading Lady (42-24766) from the 500th BG, piloted by Maj Wilbur 'Barney' Hurlbutt, was rammed between the nose and the No 3 engine over Okazaki, south-east of Nagoya, by 1Lt Minoru Shirota of the 55th Sentai. Sgt Harold T Hedges, the tail gunner and only survivor, reported their last seconds in the doomed bomber;

'We slid out of the formation and fell 5000 ft. We levelled out for just a second, the right side exploded and the aeroplane rolled over on its back and went into a spin. Just as it rolled over, it threw me out of my escape hatch. I opened my 'chute right after I went out and I was watching the ship spin down. Two Jap fighters came in strafing me and I lost sight of the ship, and that was the last time I saw it, or any of the crew.'

The big aircraft crashed into Matsudaira village, in Aichi prefecture, probably the result of an accidental collision rather than an intentional ramming. Shirota parachuted out, but died of his injuries the following day. It was his fourth, and final, B-29 victory.

Another casualty of the mission was *Joker's Wild* (42-24626) of the 497th BG, flown by 1Lt John W Lawson. Radio contact with other bombers suddenly ceased, and the aircraft was listed as missing in action,

Maj Wilbur 'Barney' Hurlbutt (second from left) was the pilot of *The Leading Lady*, an 882nd BS/500th BG aircraft. It was rammed down by 1Lt Minoru Shirota of the 55th Sentai (*Y Kumoi*)

The final resting place of *The Leading Lady* ('Z-22') was this clearing in a pine forest at Matsudaira village, in Aichi prefecture (*Y Kumoi*)

presumed to have been brought down by fighters. It may have been rammed by 1Lt Toshiro Wakui of the 56th Sentai, who was killed over Nagoya – he was posthumously promoted to major. His colleague, Sgt Yoshio Takamuki, returned from combat with the tip of his left wing broken off.

Two more B-29s, *Jumbo, King of the Show* (42-63418) of the 497th BG and *Adam's Eve* (42-24600) of the 500th BG, were lost when they were forced to ditch on the return flight. Only five crewmen from *Jumbo* were rescued – the remaining crewmen perished.

Superfortress gunners claimed 14 fighters shot down, 14 probables and 20 damaged, but in reality JAAF losses amounted to only two pilots killed – the army pilots in turn claimed an impossible 17 victories. JNAF claims and losses are unknown. Maj Furukawa, CO of the 56th Sentai, recalled the combat;

Joker's Wild belonged to the 871st BS/497th BG, and it may have been the victim of a ramming attack on 3 January 1945 (*Josh Curtis*)

1Lt Fujitaro Ito claimed two B-29 victories on 3 January 1945, and received more than 80 hits for his trouble. A sword was an officer's symbol of authority, much like a British officer's swagger stick, and was often carried into combat. Ito survived the war with the rank of captain. According to his Bukosho citation, he achieved 17 B-29 victories and damaged a further 20 (*F Ito*)

'On that day we started to climb to about 9000-10,000 m after we overflew Nagoya, and turned west because the jet stream would push us eastward. At that altitude, ice crystals twinkled and streamed over the fuselage to the tips of the wings. We felt the bitter cold. The oxygen flow meter indicated the highest marking. The engine was revolving at 2400 rpm but the control stick was heavy. We had to be most careful as the aeroplanes tended to descend. Once we had lost altitude, we would not be able to make attacks. We waited for B-29s coming in.

'Soon, engagements started with a first echelon of ten B-29s. As other B-29 groups came in, one after the other, the sky was painted with numberless white contrails streaming out from enemy and friendly aeroplanes. I have no words to describe its fierceness.'

9 JANUARY 1945

Every time the Americans tried to knock out the aircraft engine factory at target 357, the results were dismal. The two biggest obstacles they faced were not enemy fighters or flak, but bad weather and a tremendously powerful jet stream. Weather aircraft were sent over in advance to predict conditions, but this method was flawed for the crews could report optimum conditions when they were up, but six hours later the targets would be clouded over.

The powerful jet stream was menacing, with freezing winds of anything from 100 to 200 mph roaring out of Siberia. The buffeting of the aircraft interfered with the bombardier's Norden bombsight, and with the wind behind its back, the B-29 was going too fast for the bombardier to line up his target.

On 9 January 1945, the 73rd BW sent up 72 aircraft for the fifth attempt at knocking out Musashino. Again, heavy clouds and powerful winds interfered with precision bombing. The 10th Fighter Division HQ announced an air raid at 1350 hrs, and the first wave of B-29s arrived over Tokyo via Shizuoka, Kumagaya and Shimodate, while the second and third waves of more than 20 B-29s arrived via Shizuoka, Kofu and Hachioji. A very strong wind was blowing over Tokyo, and air defence staff knew it was causing havoc to the massed formations overhead. The cities of Yokohama, Fujisawa and Numazu were bombed.

Eighteen Superfortresses made it over the primary target and were forced to bomb by radar, while the remaining 34 attacked secondary targets. The results were all the same – disappointing.

The 47th Sentai at Narimasu airfield was waiting for the enemy to pass their way. Sgt Masumi Yuki was determined to destroy an intruder, and he duly rammed a B-29 flying at the left end of a formation passing over his airfield. A newspaper photographer happened to be visiting the base

This photograph was taken from Narimasu airfield by a newspaper reporter, and it shows the ramming attack by Sgt Masumi Yuki of the 47th Sentai. The crippled Superfortress was brought down by a gaggle of other 'Tojos' (K Osuo)

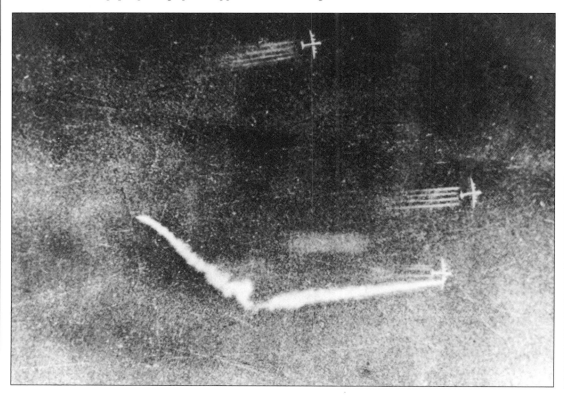

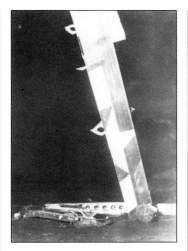

The wing of Maj Joe P Baird's aircraft imbedded itself in a field at Kodaira village, Tokyo. It belonged to the 869th BS (*Y Kumoi*)

Miss BEHAVIN from the 871st BS/ 497th BG was rammed twice and forced to ditch, with all hands lost, on 9 January 1945

when the raid occurred, and he snapped a picture of the ramming high overhead. Sgt Yuki was killed instantly and his body was found north-west of Tokyo near the torn-off engine of his intended victim. The crippled bomber fled for the open sea pursued by other 'Tojos' from the unit, led by Capt Yasuo Mazaki.

Amongst the pursuing pack was WO Takashi Awamura, one of the most skilled pilots in the 47th, and a talented inventor. He had made a flight calculator and a device which could measure the shooting range against the Superfortress, and he had also constructed a model of the airfield to help night take-offs and landings. As Awamura closed on the B-29 that Yuki had rammed, he noticed that its guns remained strangely silent. With his propeller, he sawed through his opponent's giant flaps, and the Superfortress fell into a dive off the coast of Choshi Point, while Awamura took to his parachute – he was never recovered. Japanese newspapers reported the following day that two B-29s had been shot down off Choshi Point.

The 244th Sentai were reportedly involved in a number of rammings on this day, 2Lt Mitsuyuki Tange probably hitting B-29 42-24772 of the 497th BG, for his 'Tony' crashed at Kodaira-Cho, west of Tokyo. The B-29's crew reported being at 30,000 ft when two 'Tojos' came in from 12 o'clock high and severely damaged '772, flown by Maj Joe Baird. It dropped out of formation and fell about 3000 ft, then was lost from view in the clouds. WO Gannoshin Sato, who witnessed this attack, stated;

'The B-29 was flying as "Tail End Charlie" at the right end in an eight-aeroplane formation. Tange smashed into the left outside engine from straight above. The B-29's wing was covered with flames, and it disintegrated. After crashing into a field, the bomber burned for half-an-hour.'

CHAPTER TWO

2Lt Shoichi Takayama may also have clipped this bomber north of Musashino – he parachuted to safety from his damaged fighter.

Another victim of a ramming was *Miss BEHAVIN* (42-24655) from the 497th BG, flown by 1Lt Ben Crowell. Capt Walter Young in *Waddy's Wagon* (42-24598) tried to cover for his crippled wingmate as they headed out of the target area but eventually lost them. Young's aircraft had also sustained hits from enemy fighters, and he in turn eventually ditched his aeroplane into the sea. Both crews were lost.

Capt Teruhiko Kobayashi and his wingman, Cpl Kiyoshi Ando, attacked a three-aircraft B-29 formation over the Edo river. The latter pilot claimed one destroyed, but gunners hit his aircraft's engine and radiator, and he was forced to make an emergency landing at Narimasu airfield. Flying eastward, Kobayashi pursued an eight-strong formation over Choshi Point, but the B-29s threw up a wall of fire and the young CO's 'Tony' took a hit. He made an emergency landing at Katori naval airfield.

Other members of the 244th Sentai who claimed kills were 2Lt Chuichi Ichikawa, who damaged an engine on a B-29 in a three-aircraft formation over Tokyo, and Cpl Shoichi Suzuki, who reported a victory over the capital.

The Japanese Navy's 302nd Kokutai also claimed four damaged and one victory after the army pilots chased the enemy into the naval zone. CPO Kazuo Fukuda, flying an 'Irving', claimed his victory over the Kanto (Tokyo) Plains. No pilots were lost from the 302nd.

The 73rd BW lost six B-29s during the course of the mission.

27 JANUARY 1945

The bloodiest engagement for the 73rd BW up to this point took place on 27 January 1945. The mission had all the features of a B-29 crewman's worst nightmare – poor weather, intense flak, a horde of angry fighters and target 357. With each unsuccessful mission to obliterate the engine plant at Musashino, morale plummeted.

A Japanese fighter pulls contrails at 30,000 ft as he intercepts B-29s from the 498th BG over Nagoya on 14 January 1945 (*Josh Curtis*)

Haley's Comet of the 870th BS/497th BG was shot down on 27 January 1945

Japanese twin-engined nightfighters, with their obliquely-mounted 20 mm cannon, would co-ordinate their attacks with ground searchlights to shoot up into the bellies of B-29s. This was the ideal method of attacking a Superfortress at night, but was very difficult in practice

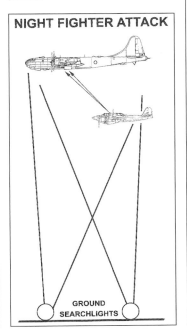

NIGHT FIGHTER ATTACK

GROUND SEARCHLIGHTS

Two Superfortresses acting as weather ships took off an hour ahead of the wing formation, their job being to determine meteorological conditions over Nagoya and Tokyo.

Seventy-six Superfortresses left Saipan, but only 64 made it to Japan. The 497th BG led the way, making landfall from Enshu Nada on a curved approach over Hamamatsu to Kofu. Its 17 B-29s, commanded by Col Robert Morgan in *Dauntless Dotty* (42-24592), were also the first to draw fire, courtesy of the 244th Sentai from Chofu.

One of the first bombers to be downed was *Haley's Comet* (42-24616), piloted by 1Lt Walter McDonnell. Battered by flak and fighters, the B-29 dropped behind the formation with its bomb-bay on fire. The bomber was most likely attacked by an 'Irving' nightfighter from the Navy's 302nd Kokutai, whose pilot manoeuvred underneath the Superfortress and fired into its belly with a pair of obliquely-mounted 20 mm cannon.

The attacker did not survive to savour his achievement. The 'Irving' was vulnerable to defensive fire from the B-29s in a daylight attack, and two examples were shot down. The fighter flown by PO2/c Kiyoho Takada, with Ens Mitsuo Kimura as observer, crashed into the Tenryu river near Hamamatsu after reporting one B-29 shot down, while WO Hisao Komori and PO2/c Toshio Hayakawa plunged into the Oi river, in central Shizuoka prefecture. They too had claimed a Kill. S/Sgt Vere D Carpenter and Sgt Fred Lodovici bailed out of *Haley's Comet*, were captured, and survived the war. Their aircraft crashed at Ishino, in Chiba prefecture.

WERE WOLF (42-63423), piloted by Capt Elmer G Hahn, may have also fallen victim to an 'Irving', for it took a hit in the bomb-bay between Hamamatsu and Kofu and broke in two. Four crewmen died in the crash near Fujimiya, in Shizuoka prefecture. No parachutes were spotted, and it was thought that no one had got out, but seven crewman had in fact managed to escape – three of them died when their 'chutes malfunctioned, however. Four men were captured – Capt Hahn, 2Lts Eugene J Redinger (co-pilot), Herbert Edman (flight engineer) and Sgt Clifford A Myra

The wreckage of *Haley's Comet* is examined by Japanese troops at Ishino, Shisui, in Chiba prefecture (*Y Kumoi*)

(gunner), who were sent to Tokyo. Sgt Myra was transferred to an army hospital in Saitama prefecture, but died from burns on 10 February. The three other prisoners were burned to death at Shibuya army prison in a B-29 fire raid on 26 May.

1Lt Stanley H Samuelson was the pilot of 'Z-12' (42-24692) from the 500th BG, one of the two weather aircraft on the mission. He wrote in his diary;

'After our two-ship formation left the mainland of Japan, I tuned in our B-channel on the VHF radio just in time to hear the large formation behind us talking from one plane to the other over the target. It was a tragic conversation that I shall never forget. Some were reporting their buddies going down in flames. Others were yelling for "Superdumbos", which are search planes sent out by us to spot aircraft that have ditched. Others were begging for protection and cover from other B-29s. Someone yelled over the radio, "Let's get the hell out of this mess!"'

The short stretch from Kofu to Otsuki, on the beeline path to Tokyo, was only 20 miles long, but it must have felt like a thousand while under intense attack. Col Robert Haynes and the crew of *THUMPER (42-24623)* from the 497th BG felt the full brunt of the assault by 'Tonys' from the 244th Sentai and 'Tojos' from the 47th.

1Lt Chuichi Ichikawa, the second highest B-29 killer in the 244th, may have clashed with 'Pappy' Haynes, for his division followed the lone Superfortress, which had one engine out, but refrained from closing due to the aircraft's tremendous defensive firepower. Mad as hell, Col Haynes banked his aircraft to turn into them. 'Hang on, boys, we're going after those bastards!' he shouted over the interphone.

Piloted by Capt Elmer G Hahn, *WERE WOLF*, of the 870th BS/497th BG, was hit by fighters over the target on 27 January 1945. A fire broke out in the bomb-bay, and then the B-29 exploded

Suddenly a large flock of 'Tonys' came tearing in from the opposite direction. It was a trap. But the Superfortress with the Walt Disney cartoon rabbit painted on the nose proved it could defend itself, repelling attack after attack, and claiming six victories and more than a dozen damaged. Ichikawa may have claimed *THUMPER* as a victory, but the valiant crew brought her safely home.

As Col Morgan's flock fought their way from Kofu to Tokyo (a distance of only 60 miles), they were spotted by the 244th Sentai's CO, Capt Kobayashi, and his wingman Cpl Ando as they patrolled at 10,000 m over Hachioji, east of Kofu and Otsuki. Judging that the 14-strong B-29 formation would turn right to proceed to Tokyo, Kobayashi and Ando turned to block the enemy's course. Kobayashi calculated the distance, angle of attack and time to catch the formation from behind. With his

Walt Disney cartoon characters adorned quite a few B-29s, including *THUMPER* of the 870th BS/497th BG. Note the small Japanese flags denoting the gunners' victories – they claimed six kills on the mission of 27 January 1945. After 40 missions, *THUMPER* was the first to return home to the US, where it went on a bond-selling tour (*Josh Curtis*)

Capt Teruhiko Kobayashi stands by his fighter with silhouettes of some of his B-29 claims. Whenever he switched aircraft, he would have his crewchief transfer victory markings to his new mount. He rammed *Irish Lassie*, but failed to bring her down

Irish Lassie, of the 497th BG, had an incredible will to live. Rammed twice, she brought her crew home but broke up on landing and was scrapped (*Josh Curtis*)

wingman at his side, the pair dived down into the tight combat formation. The B-29 gunners threw up a wall of lead.

Irish Lassie (42-65246) was clipped by a fighter, the unidentified aircraft hitting the left wing behind the No 1 engine and rupturing a gas tank. The wounded Superfortress remained defiantly airborne, but was attracting attention. Kobayashi set his sights on *Irish Lassie* and smashed into the left stabiliser, being knocked unconscious for a few seconds. He quickly came

to and bailed out, landing safely near Tachikawa, west of target 357. Although *Irish Lassie* was claimed as a kill by several Japanese pilots, she repaid the crew by delivering them safely home. On landing, the bomber broke in two and was scrapped.

Cpl Ando rammed the fourth aircraft in the same formation, *Ghastly Goose* (42-63541) of the 497th, piloted by Capt Dale Peterson, taking the hit but surviving. Ando was not so lucky, and his Ki-61 crashed at Funabashi, in Chiba prefecture, on the north side of Tokyo Bay. The Superfortress may have suffered another ramming at the hands of Sgt Yuichi Kobayashi and observer Cpl Natsuo Koibuchi of the Hitachi Training Unit, whose 'Nick' crashed near Funabashi. Capt Peterson was escorted away from the target area by another aircraft and ditched about 250 miles from Japan, but the crew were never recovered.

Shady Lady (42-24619) almost made it to the target, but the intense fighter attacks took their toll. Capt Raymond Dauth steered his aircraft into cloud for protection, but was nevertheless rammed head-on by a 'Tojo' flown by M/Sgt Kiyoshi Suzuki of the 47th Sentai. Suzuki's aircraft crashed into a river at Oume city, Tokyo, west of target 357.

Looking up from Matsudo airbase in Chiba prefecture, groundcrewman Sgt Ryoji Harada of the 53rd Sentai wrote in his diary;

'Towards 1420 hrs a lightning flashed in the clouds when a series of thunderous roars shook the earth. The sky over Tokyo was quickly covered with black smoke, and flames were seen rising even in daylight. No aircraft were seen. Roars of B-29s were only heard over the clouds. The first B-29 formation was roaring away in a retreat over our base. When the second formation was reportedly at Otsuki, the third was coming in

Shady Lady **served with the 870th BS/497th BG until it was rammed by M/Sgt Kiyoshi Suzuki of the 47th Sentai. No one survived**

towards southern Kanto and the fourth was heading north, 50 km south of Omaezaki.'

The 498th BG's 'T-2' (42-63501), commanded by Capt Pierce Kilgo, successfully completed its bombing run over Tokyo but never made it home. The aircraft left the formation soon after departing the target area with two engines out. WO Shirobe Tanaka of the 244th Sentai had already inflicted damage on one Superfortress when he spotted Kilgo's aircraft over Haramachida, south-west of Tokyo. The 'Tony' pilot rammed his mount into the bomber's tail and he was flung out of his fighter in an unconscious state, his parachute already deployed. Coming down in Tokyo Bay, Tanaka was pulled out of the water by a fishing boat. Having suffered serious injuries, he never returned to combat. For his bravery, Tanaka was awarded the Bukosho. The B-29 crashed near the coast.

Another aircraft of the 498th also found itself in a jam. B-29 42-24767 of 1Lt William F Beyhan fought its way through the enemy gauntlet, but lost No 1 and 2 engines. A JNAF 'Irving', crewed by Ens Kisaburo Sakada and PO1/c Ryoitsu Kitagawa, attacked a nine-aircraft B-29 formation over Tokyo and left one spewing black smoke – possibly Beyhan's. The return fire from the Superfortress knocked out both engines on the Navy fighter, however, although the Japanese pilot managed to glide down to Kisarazu naval airfield at Chiba.

Beyhan radioed 1Lt John Rawlings Jr in 'T-37', telling him that his electrical system was out and that he could not transfer fuel. Rawlings followed him down through bad weather, relying on his radar. With daylight fading, Beyhan decided to ditch in the rough sea. The aircraft broke in two on impact and some of the men were seen getting into life rafts. Rawling's crew did what they could for their colleagues, throwing out an extra life raft and emergency equipment. Beyhan's crew were never seen again.

The 499th BG's 1Lt Edward G 'Snuffy' Smith and *Rover Boys Express* (42-24769) were flying their fourth mission. They had safely made it through the flak, and were just about to open the bomb-bay doors, when twin-engined fighters were spotted ahead. 'Fighters at one o'clock high, heading directly for us!' warned a voice on the interphone. And unbeknown to the B-29 crew, these Ki-45s boasted 37 mm cannon.

'Suddenly there was a tremendous explosion, a terrifying noise and fire and smoke in our front section', recalled navigator Raymond 'Hap' Halloran. 'V-27' had taken a 37 mm shell right in its nose. Smith was hit in both arms and bombardier 2Lt Robert Grace was seriously wounded. Three engines had failed, and two of them were on fire. The interphone system was destroyed and the aircraft, still fully laden with bombs, gradually began to lose altitude. Their friends in other aircraft could do nothing for them.

Trust was the bond that kept a Superfortress crew working together. Everyone depended on each other for their lives. The four gunners and the radar operator in the rear section had no idea what had happened up front. 'We would never leave the *Rover Boys* in the rear section alone in this terrifying situation', said Halloran. 'Guy Knobel, our radioman, took off his chest pack parachute so he could go through the tunnel that separated the front and rear sections of the B-29. As Guy proceeded through the tunnel, we were continuously attacked by single-engined "Tojo" fighters. We were being torn apart in the air. He was a very brave man'.

The three surviving crewmen in the rear (the tail gunner was dead in his seat) were told to bail out, along with the others. 2Lt Halloran grabbed his lunch of turkey sandwiches, took a few big bites, and jumped. All ten

The crew of *Rover Boys Express* are seen just before their departure to Saipan. 2Lt Raymond 'Hap' Halloran is standing in the centre, with pilot 1Lt Edward 'Snuffy' Smith to his left (*Hap Halloran*)

2Lt 'Hap' Halloran was the navigator on *Rover Boys Express,* and he traded salutes with Cpl Hideichi Kaiho as three Japanese fighters buzzed him as he parachuted down. Halloran and four crewmen survived captivity. In October 2000, he went back to visit the crash site of his B-29 at Ikisu village, and prayed for his colleagues who did not make it (*Hap Halloran*)

crewmen were supposed to parachute, but only seven did, and from an estimated 27,000 ft over the Tokyo plains. Halloran pulled his ripcord at around 4000 ft above the ground, losing his right flying boot in the sudden jolt.

In one of the strangest episodes of the bombing campaign, three JAAF Mansyu Ki-79 fixed-gear advanced fighter trainers circled the dangling American, making two very close passes. With nothing to lose, Halloran waved to them. Cpl Hideichi Kaiho of the 39th Training Unit acknowledged Halloran's friendly gesture with a salute on his second circuit, and two of his comrades left. Kaiho circled around for the third time, gave another salute, confirmed Halloran's landing point, then went on his way. Maj Tetsuo Watabe, Kaiho's commander, stressed the importance of military propriety in his instructions to his men. 'We have *Bushido*, just as the westerners have chivalry!'

Rover Boys Express crashed into Ikisu village near Konoike naval airfield in Ibaraki prefecture – seven civilians were killed as several houses caught fire. Four bodies were found in the wreckage of the aircraft, and another body was found in a field north of the crash site. Of the seven who

Cpl Hideichi Kaiho in March 1945. His duty on 27 January that year was to pinpoint the landing sites of B-29 crewmen. He flew an obsolete trainer armed with only one 7.7 mm machine gun. In October 2000 he shook hands with former B-29 navigator 'Hap' Halloran, whom he had spared (*H Kaiho*)

parachuted, only five survived the war – 1Lt Edward Smith, 2Lts Ray 'Hap' Halloran and James W Edwards, S/Sgt Guy H Knobel and Sgt Philip J Nicholson.

They were captured by men from the nearby naval airfield and were ill-treated by the Tokyo *Kempei Tai* – rather ironic, considering Maj Watabe's words about military propriety. 2Lt William J Franz Jr also parachuted, and was killed by angry villagers. There is evidence that 2Lt Robert L Grace was captured and was alive as of 10 March, but he was never seen again.

Mission 24 ended with nine B-29s lost by the 73rd BW. Once again, heavy cloud cover had spared the engine factory at Musashino, and the aerial armada had been forced to bomb secondary targets. However, their gunners claimed 60 kills, 17 probables and 39 damaged. This was the last mission flown solo by the 73rd.

The JAAF and JNAF fighters claimed a total of 22 B-29s destroyed for the loss of 15 or 16 aircraft. Of the ten aircraft that reportedly rammed their opponents, four pilots parachuted to safety, one got his aircraft back to base and five died.

PHASE TWO OPERATIONS

At the end of XXI Bomber Command's Phase One operation against Japan, completed with Mission 24 on 27 January 1945, the verdict was – failure. The infamous Target 357, the Musashino engine factory, was hit six times by the 73rd BW at the cost of 27 B-29s destroyed and many more damaged. Yet very little damage to the factory could be detected by photo analysis.

The failure of Phase One in the bombing campaign was attributed to Brig Gen Hansell's tactical inflexibility – he was a committed believer in high-altitude precision bombing. He was replaced by Gen Curtiss LeMay on 20 January, just as Phase One was coming to a close.

The much-needed reinforcements to hammer the Japanese mainland began to arrive in the Marianas that month. The first of the newcomers was the 313th BW, commanded by Gen John J Davies. The wing had received its combat training in Nebraska, and was shipped off to North

Maj Gen Curtiss LeMay replaced Brig Gen Haywood Hansell as head of XXI Bomber Command. Under LeMay's leadership, successful low-level fire-bombing of Japanese cities was quickly introduced (*Josh Curtis*)

Field, on Tinian. Its crews flew a number of practice missions in January, bombing the enemy strongholds on Truk and Iwo Jima. These dress rehearsals were a prelude to conducting joint operations with the now battle-scarred 73rd BW.

The first combined mission (Mission 26) took place on 4 February, the bombers heading for Kobe, considered to be Japan's greatest port. It was famous for its ship-building and marine cargo facilities, and major railways and roads led to the crowded city. As a result of the mission, more than two-and-a-half million square feet of target area was destroyed or damaged by incendiary and fragmentation bombs, at the cost of just two B-29s.

The biggest raid to date occurred six days later, with 118 B-29s taking to the air and 98 reaching Japan. Their target was the Nakajima aircraft factory at Ota, in Gunma prefecture, west of Tokyo. The factory was churning out the Ki-84 *Hayates* for the JAAF.

At 1315 hrs (Japan time) the radar site on Hachijo Island picked up the B-29 lead formation. After the Americans passed east of the Izu Islands, the 10th Fighter Division's plotters judged that the Americans would not take the usual western route via Mt Fuji to Tokyo, and directed the main fighter force to the east of the capital. As expected, the Superfortresses came in from Kashima Nada.

The air raid alert was also received by the JNAF, which quickly scrambled 74 fighters (mostly 'Jacks') of the 302nd Kokutai from Atsugi airfield. The

2Lt Makoto Ogawa was the top B-29 hunter in the 70th Sentai, claiming seven Superfortresses and two P-51s flying the 'Tojo'. He was awarded the Bukosho and survived the war (*Y Izawa*)

83

Navy's 252nd Kokutai was making its combat debut in the home defence role on this day, the unit controlling five fighter squadrons with a total of 240 Zeroes. Despite these seemingly impressive numbers, the 252nd was still very much in training, and only a few veterans took off from Katori and Tateyama.

Eighty-four B-29s were able to bomb the primary target, while fourteen hit secondary targets. No fewer than 87 'Franks' were destroyed on the factory production line, as well as 11 of the 37 factory buildings. After bombing Ota, the formations made a wide right turn and headed east towards Mito, in Ibaraki prefecture, and out to sea.

But it had not all gone the Americans' way. Aerial opposition had come from the 'Tojo'-equipped 70th Sentai, based at Kashiwa airfield, whose top B-29 specialist was WO Makoto Ogawa of the 3rd squadron. He and his colleagues were veterans who had clashed with B-29s over Manchuria. The 70th had been patrolling at a height of 10,000 m over Mt Fuji when they heard that the B-29s were heading for Tokyo from the east. Taking advantage of the powerful jet stream, they had sped towards Ota.

Ogawa managed to catch the second tail formation over Ota and made a straight diving attack, slicing through the combat box and then making a second attack on the same formation from below. Then, the bomb-bay doors of his target started to open, so he quickly fired a burst. Ogawa's bullets hit home and there was a tremendous explosion. He backed off and saw two B-29s going down – his wingman reported that the wreckage from his first victim had hit another aircraft, and both bombers crashed.

Elsewhere, *Slick's Chicks* (42-24784) of the 505th BG, piloted by Capt Carmel Slaughter Jr, may have crossed paths with 2Lt Toshizo Kurai of the 1st Training Unit, based at Sagami, in Kanagawa prefecture. With

Slick's Chicks, which belonged to the 483rd BS/505th BG, was rammed by 1Lt Toshizo Kurai on 10 February 1945, according to official Japanese records. The impact caused the bomber to collide with another B-29 within its formation. 313th BW records state that *Slick's Chicks* collided with *Deaner Boy*, and both aircraft were lost

'Follow me today!' were the last words spoken by 1Lt Heikichi Yoshizawa of the 47th Sentai. He rammed his 'Tojo' into a B-29 on 10 February 1945 over Ota and was killed. In this photograph, Yoshizawa is seen standing in front of a Ki-84 *Hayate*

four B-29 victories to his credit, Kurai plunged head-on into a diamond formation of Superfortresses over the target. *Slick's Chick* then collided with *Deaner Boy* (42-24815), flown by 1Lt Owen Barnhart Jr, and both bombers went crashing down into Takashima village, in Gunma prefecture. The wreckage burned for three days. Kurai, who was killed in the attack, was credited with two victories.

1Lt Heikichi Yoshizawa of the 47th Sentai knew he would bring down a Superfortress that day. Before setting off for combat, he had pinned a small cloth good-luck doll on his flying suit, and told his colleague, 2Lt Ryozo Ban, 'Follow me today!' 'Yes sir, I will. I will follow you to heaven or hell!', his subordinate had replied. The pair jumped into their 'Tojos' and flew to Ota, where they immediately spotted B-29s.

The Americans saw the 'Tojos' and started to spray gunfire in their direction. Yoshizawa pulled ahead of Ban and flew into the formation upside down, turned himself upright, and skimmed over the tops of the bombers, just ten metres above them. His aircraft struck one of the B-29s and he was killed. Ban's engine was hit and he had to make an emergency landing at Shimodate airfield, in Ibaraki prefecture.

Cpl Saburo Umehara of the 244th Sentai's Toppu unit was also killed when he rammed an opponent over Mt Tsukuba, in Ibaraki. A photograph of his mother Chie was found in the soil at Shimodate where his 'Tony' had ploughed its way into the ground. The Army erected a wooden monument at the crash site.

Mission 29 had seen the Americans' suffer their biggest loss in the campaign to date – 12 B-29s, seven of them ditched. Japanese defence forces claimed 21 victories (the JAAF 15, JNAF three and anti-aircraft three). Seven JAAF pilots had been killed, three of them in ramming attacks.

19 FEBRUARY 1945

Mission 37 on 19 February was another joint raid by the 73rd and 313th BWs, timed to coincide with the invasion of Iwo Jima. The priority target, known so well by all aircrew as target 357, was to receive a visit from a force of 150 aircraft.

As usual, the Japanese were waiting for them, and Musashino was clouded over. Not one bomb fell on the engine plant, and the factory kept on working. However, secondary targets were saturated by 131 aircraft.

2Lt Osamu Hirose of the 53rd Sentai was leading four aircraft as they waited for the enemy near Mt Fuji. Before long, a 12-strong formation of Superfortresses was spotted heading east away from the mountain at an altitude of 8300 m. Immediately, Hirose ordered an attack from the rear and above, and he managed to damage the second aircraft in the second formation. When he pulled up from his dive, he noticed another enemy

This aerial view of Nagoya, taken from a 874th BS B-29 cruising at 26,200 ft on 15 February 1945, shows the Mitsubishi engine factory on the upper right just prior to being bombed. Only one B-29 was lost on this mission (*Josh Curtis*)

formation of eight B-29s approaching from behind him, west of Otsuki. Unfortunately he had used up all his ammunition, and the right engine of his Ki-45 had taken hits – it was belching white smoke. Suddenly, B-29 42-24692 of the 500th BG, piloted by Capt Stanley H Samuelson, came into view.

Hirose shouted into the intercom to his backseat observer, 'Kato, let's go in!' Cpl Kimio Kato furiously tapped out a message to his base. 'Hirose is going in right now!' From 29,000 ft, the 'Nick' dropped on the B-29 like a guillotine blade, striking 'Z-12' at the top of the fuselage behind the wings, cutting it in two.

The force of the high-speed impact was terrific, Kato seeing something like a 'large tin roof' flash in front of his face seconds before he passed out after hearing a deafening roar. The force of the impact threw him out of the rear cockpit. The static line from his parachute pack, connected to the seat, automatically yanked his parachute out, and the unconscious crewman floated down. His 'chute snagged on a tree, breaking his descent. Amazingly he had survived.

In a windowless compartment in the B-29, radio operator S/Sgt Robert P Evans never knew what hit them. 'I kept thinking, this couldn't be happening to me!' recalled Evans, ultimately the only survivor from the bomber. He was thrown out and parachuted into captivity. Sgt H Weiser did not survive his parachute descent and was buried at Jofukuji Temple. Badly burned in the collision, Robert J Janecek had also succeeded in jumping from the wrecked B-29, and was captured the following day. Sent to Tokyo, he died at the 1st temporary army hospital in Tokyo on

On 19 February 1945 Capt Stanley H Samuelson's B-29 was rammed over the target by the 53rd Sentai's 2Lt Osamu Hirose (see the cover artwork for a depiction of this attack). Capt Samuelson is standing on the far right, while the sole survivor of the collision, S/Sgt Paul Evans, is squatting second from the right in the front row (*Len Chaloux*)

Members of the 53rd Sentai's ramming unit are the subjects of this photograph, taken in late 1944. The pilot third from the right is Sgt Masami Sawamoto, who was killed ramming Maj Robert Goldsworthy's B-29 over Tokyo on 3 December 1944. The tall pilot standing next to Sawamoto on the right, is Cpl Kenji Yamada, who was killed when he rammed *SUPER Wabbit* on 19 February 1945

6 March from a lack of medical attention. The wreckage came down on Nishihara village, in Yamanashi prefecture.

Cpl Kenji Yamada, also of the 53rd Sentai, was flying in a four-strong force led by 2Lt Aoki towards Tokyo Bay. He spotted a formation of 12 B-29s heading eastward, and each pilot picked out a target. 1Lt Martin Nicholson, at the controls of *SUPER Wabbit* (42-65222) from the 499th BG, did not realise that Cpl Yamada had chosen him as his victim. The 'Nick' pilot made a steep turn and headed straight for the incoming B-29s over Lake Kawaguchi.

An eyewitness recalled the ramming incident. 'I saw a fire in the southern sky just as if a match had been struck. The Superfortress was sliced in half, and each section came down one kilometre apart'. None of the crew survived, Nicholson and five others being found in the forward section, and the rest of the crew in the wreckage of the rear. The bodies were buried in a local cemetery.

Maj Masato Kodama, the last commander of the 53rd Sentai, remarked on why some pilots resorted to ramming;

'The twin-seat fighter *Toryu*, using two types of guns – fixed cannons and a circular gun mounted in the rear seat – was a fighter intended to attack enemy aircraft from below. When attacking a B-29 at a height of about 10,000 m, the Japanese aircraft would be near its performance limit.

'The pilots would meet with many difficulties whilst try to perform these interceptions. Unskilled pilots would try to improve the Ki-45's flying performance by decreasing equipment and trying to ram their targets.'

The main body of the 19 February raid (about 90 B-29s in six echelons) was spotted by JAAF fighters at a height of 8000 m over Otsuki. At about

Yamada's victim (*SUPER Wabbit* of the 877th BS/499th BG) is seen some weeks prior to its demise on 19 February 1945

1450 hrs, two large balls of fire dropped on the Yotsuya 7th Primary School at Shinjuku, in Tokyo. The rear portion of a B-29 fuselage hit the ground, while the other section landed on the roof. Three bodies were found on the roof and two on the ground. Newspaper reporters gathered at the scene, and shortly thereafter a young pilot arrived. 'I am the pilot that shot down this B-29', said Cpl Tomonobu Matsueda of the 244th Sentai. 'I have come to see the crash site'.

Matsueda told the reporters that he had spotted a formation of ten aircraft, and made repeated attacks before the Superfortress fell out of formation. He fired in a straight diving attack, and the bomber's nose broke off and disintegrated. His aircraft was hit by return fire, and he made an emergency landing on an army drill ground at Shibuya. Getting out of his 'Tony', he had run all the way to the crash scene. Matsueda's victim was 'Z-31' (42-63494) of the 500th BG. Only Sgts Edward H McGrath and Lee M Johnston survived by parachuting, and they were liberated after the war.

The 244th Sentai claimed two B-29s destroyed and four damaged that day, while overall, JAAF units were credited with the destruction of 21 B-29s for the loss of four fighters. The JNAF's claims are unknown, but the 302nd Kokutai lost two 'Judys' and three aircrew.

Capt Stanley Samuelson, who was killed in a ramming attack during the mission, had written a last diary entry;

'It is so very hard living under these circumstances. It's humanly impossible to get used to seeing your buddies go down all the time, so most of us try to ignore the fact . . . it's funny in a way, we don't pray that everyone comes out okay, all we ask is that they come out alive.'

The wreckage of 878th BS/499th BG B-29 42-24754, flown by 2Lt John K Ellington, litters the downtown area of Sakaisuji, in Osaka. It was shot down during the night mission of 13-14 March 1945 almost certainly by M/Sgt Tadao Sumi. This was the only aircraft lost over Japan that night (*Y Kumoi*)

Cpl Kenji Yamada, who was also killed in a ramming attack, had also kept a diary, and had composed a poem in traditional style;

'Why do I spare my life for the Emperor? Young and live cherry flowers have their significance of lives because they are gone early.

'I have been chosen as a member of a special attack unit. What a great honour it is! I feel a joy as I was born as a man. What a pleasure it is to ram! (Signed) Imperial Army Corporal Kenji Yamada, 22, Shinten Unit.'

Mission 37 ended with a total of six B-29s lost (two of them rammed over the target).

16-17 MARCH 1945

With the daylight precision-bombing raids not proving to be cost-effective, a directive was issued on 19 February for more fire-bomb testing. Six days later Tokyo was hit by 201 B-29s in the largest aerial arson attack to date. The results were formidable – nearly a square mile of metropolitan Tokyo went up in flames. Gen LeMay was now convinced that Tokyo, Osaka, Kobe and Nagoya could be gutted by low-level fire-bomb attacks.

He wanted to put as many incendiaries on target as his aircraft could carry, and his staff decided that to make this possible, all bombers would have to be stripped of unnecessary weight. They would carry out a night assault, and because Japanese nightfighters posed little threat, all guns and ammunition would be discarded. Only the few pathfinder aircraft were to be fully armed. To insure accuracy, they would bomb from 5000-9000 ft. The plan was radical, and it was the most difficult order Gen LeMay would ever have to give.

On the night of 9-10 March, 325 B-29s prepared to head for Tokyo. Many of the crews were furious with LeMay for sending them out unarmed at medium altitude, and swearing could be heard all over the base. Most thought it was a suicide mission.

That night, a total of 279 aircraft bombed from an altitude of 4900-9200 ft. Aerial photographs taken the following day revealed that more than 15 square miles of Tokyo had been burned to the ground. LeMay's daring plan had been vindicated. On the down-side, 14 B-29s were lost, the most on any mission undertaken by XXI Bomber Command to date.

One week later, on the night of 16-17 March, Mission 43 was despatched to Kobe, some 330 Superfortresses being tasked with fire-bombing the port. They were met over the target by 'Tojos' from the 246th Sentai, based at Taisho airfield, in Osaka. M/Sgt Kenji Fujimoto and Sgt Yukio Ikuta both rammed a B-29 and survived – it was Fujimoto's second ramming, for three nights earlier he had successfully brought down another B-29 following a collision.

Tall In The Saddle **belonged to the 93rd BS/19th BG, and it was one of 14 B-29s lost on the mission to Tokyo on the night of 9-10 March. The bomber's pilot was Capt Gordon L Master (*Maru*)**

Curious sailors from a nearby naval base examine the tail section of *Tall In The Saddle* (*K Osuo*)

Naval officer Lt(jg) Teishiro Shiono examines the nose wheel of *Tall In The Saddle* (*K Osuo*)

Lt(jg) Shiono also crawled through the shattered rear fuselage section of *Tall In The Saddle,* before emerging out of the remarkably intact tailgunner's compartment *(K Osuo)*

An engine from *Tall In the Saddle* (*Y Kumoi*)

At dawn, Capt Noboru Nagasue's four 'Tonys' from the 56th Sentai had been scrambled in response to the Kobe raid – Capt Junichi Ogata's flight of four aircraft took off 80 minutes later to avoid flying in an overlapping air defence zone in darkness. Once over Kobe, Ogata sent a radio report to Maj Haruyoshi Furukawa, CO of the air group at Itami airfield (situated 15 miles south-west of the port city). 'Enemy bombers are clearly lit up by an inferno on the ground in the urban area'. Then another report came in. 'One plane destroyed! I'll keep on attacking!' This was the last message that would ever be heard from Ogata.

M/Sgt Kenji Fujimoto of the 246th Sentai rammed a B-29 during the night action of 13-14 March over Osaka, and then successfully took to his parachute. Three nights later he again rammed and survived, and Fujimoto received the Bukosho for these outstanding feats of bravery. His luck finally ran out on 14 August (just one day before the surrender announcement), when he was shot down and killed by P-51s (*K Osuo*)

Back at Itami, WO Kuniyoshi Hasegawa and some of the groundcrew at the airfield saw a spot of light streaming like a shooting star into a B-29 that was lit up by two searchlights. Seconds later a huge fireball erupted. They had almost certainly witnessed Ogata's final attack on the American formation.

Maj Furukawa recalled the destruction of the bombing;

'The roaring flames from Kobe city shot skywards, inviting boiling clouds and strong winds. With the wind blowing from the west, there was a menacing atmosphere prevailing all over the area.'

Officially, no B-29s were shot down by Japanese fighters that night, although three were lost on the mission. However, one Superfortress had been rammed by Ogata, who slammed into Maj Bob Fitzgerald's 'Z-8' (42-24849) of the 500th BG two miles north of Kobe. The bomber went down near a PoW camp. Two crewmen, 2Lt Robert W Nelson and S/Sgt Algy Stanley Augunas, were captured. They were convicted in a two-hour trial in Osaka and executed on 18 July, less than a month before the war ended.

Down in the PoW camp, Friar Marcian Pellet, a Franciscan missionary, saw the B-29 falling out of the sky at about 0400 hrs. One of the victims of the crash was the co-pilot, 2Lt Robert Copeland. 'When the Jap soldiers failed to bury the bodies, we internees secretly buried them', Friar Pellet wrote to Lt Copeland's mother, Norma, after the war. 'We later erected crosses with their names and marked the spots clearly. Rest assured that we fathers in the camp prayed at the graves, and also in our masses, for the men'.

Capt Ogata had claimed eight bomber kills over Burma during his time with the 77th Sentai, followed by four B-29 victories and five damaged during his home defence service. Respected as a good leader, he had gone on his final sortie soon after his daughter was born. One of Ogata's flight

Capt Junichi Ogata rammed his 'Tony' into Maj Bob Fitzgerald's B-29 on 17 March 1945 and was killed (*Koji Takaki*)

The crew of Maj Bob Fitzgerald's B-29 pose for a standard group shot at the start of their operational tour. Any B-29 crewmen captured in the Kobe area were treated as a war criminals, and two men from this crew parachuted, were convicted in a two-hour trial and immediately executed (*Bill Copeland*)

B-29 Gunner Loses Beer Over Kobe

A B-29 BASE, Tinian, March 18 - Sunday - Irish Sergt. Walter C. Calhoun of Lakeville, Ill, gunner on a B-29 attacking Kobe yesterday, didn't celebrate St. Patrick's Day like he hoped.

Four cans of beer he had cooling in the camera hatch fell through the opening over the target.

This short clipping from a US newspaper reported the 'tragic loss' for Sgt Walter Calhoun on the night mission of 16-17 March 1945 over Kobe. The story fails to mention that three B-29s were also lost on this mission

boots with his name on it was discovered in the wreckage of the B-29, and his body was eventually found when crows began to circle it. He was posthumously promoted to lieutenant colonel.

Ogata had chosen the method of his spectacular demise, for his 56th Sentai had not formed a dedicated flight to undertake such ramming attacks – these were set up in all the JAAF air defence squadrons deployed around Tokyo, and by the 4th Sentai at Ozuki, in western Honshu. A ramming was carried out by a 56th pilot only when *he* decided to do so.

Mission 43 burned out nearly three square miles of Kobe. Although only three B-29s were lost, the JAAF claimed a fictitious 19 kills for the loss of at least one aircraft.

7 APRIL 1945

Mission 58 signalled the first time that the 73rd BW had bombed the home islands with the benefit of fighter escorts. Up until now, the USAAF's island bases had been situated too far away from Japan to allow single-engined fighters to protect the bombers attacking key targets such as Tokyo, Kobe and Nagoya. However, the recent capture of Okinawa (and in particular Ie Shima) and Iwo Jima, and the arrival of long-range P-47N and P-51D fighters in the Central Pacific meant that fighters would at last be able to venture over mainland Japan.

Initially, only fighter pilots with 600-700 hours of frontline flying were picked for this mission, while second and third-stringers begged and pleaded with their seniors to be assigned as stand-ins. Upon hearing this, morale amongst the B-29 crews immediately shot up.

The target on 7 April was a familiar one – the engine plant at Musashino, which was about to be hit by the 73rd BW for a tenth time! Of the 107 B-29s that took off, 103 reached the Japanese mainland, escorted by 96 of the 106 P-51D Mustangs (from the 15th and 21st FGs) that VIIth Fighter Command had sortied from Iwo Jima behind a B-29 navigation aircraft. About 100 miles from Tokyo, the Mustangs rendezvoused with the large Superfortress formation as it commenced its bombing run. The P-51 pilots had to perform a series of scissor manoeuvres so as to avoid getting ahead of the B-29s, and they made landfall with Mt Fuji towering over the horizon, marking their turning point. The final stretch would see the large formation run the fighter gauntlet to Tokyo.

Capt Robert 'Todd' Moore of the 78th FS called out the first bogie when he spotted a twin-engined 'Nick' at low altitude over Tokyo Bay. However, the Mustang pilots smelled a decoy and stayed in formation. The Japanese pilots were both surprised and alarmed to see fighter escorts, and they did their best to ignore them, focusing their attention instead exclusively on the bombers.

One such pilot was 2Lt Satohide Kohatsu of the 244th Sentai's 2nd Chutai, who recalls the ramming he was involved in;

'I took off as part of the flight led by Capt Goro Takeda. My engine soon began running rough, however, and I signalled to the lead aeroplane that I would part from the formation. I decided to patrol over Chofu at 5000 m, and I soon spotted a B-29 formation over Kawasaki. In order to get into a favourable position from which to attack, I tried to climb as the B-29s came straight for my fighter. There was an altitude difference of about 500 m between us. Prior to taking off, we had decided that there was

The infamous Target 357, in Tokyo, is seen on a rare clear day from an altitude of 15,700 ft during the bombing mission of 7 April 1945. The Nakajima engine factory was finally knocked out on this day, on the tenth attempt. 7 April also saw P-51 fighter escorts make their operational debut over the Japanese capital (*Josh Curtis*)

no other attack tactic against B-29s as effective as the interception from straight above or from slightly below and ahead. My altitude was not sufficient for an attack from above, so I went in firing from the front and below the bomber.

'Moments later, the right wing of my aeroplane came off at the root. My aircraft went into a horizontal spin to the left, circling around the tail. It could not be accelerated, nor controlled. Hot radiator water blew out of the engine and the windshield was blackened by hot oil. It blew against my face and I could hardly open my eyes. I was in total darkness, and could not see through the canopy. I knew I was alive, however. I tried to stand up to bail out, but was pulled back by an enormous force.'

In a desperate attempt to free himself, Kohatsu placed his right foot on the stick, locked his left foot underneath the edge of the canopy railing, and shoved both hands against the top of the canopy with all his might. Suddenly, his body was sucked out of the cockpit. He could see one of his flight boots dancing over him as he fell. Looking up, he also saw a group of B-29s passing overhead, and some gunners firing at him. 'What a big aeroplane!' he recalled. 'Our fighters were so small. It was like an eagle versus a sparrow. And there were far more B-29s than our fighters'.

The B-29 that Kohatsu had hit was *Mrs. TITTYMOUSE* (42-65212) of the 498th BG, piloted by 1Lt John O Wise. While descending in his parachute, Kohatsu saw another B-29 slowly spinning down, the shattered bomber spiralling two-and-a-half times before hitting the ground, rammed down by 2Lt Takashi Kawano, Kohatsu's roommate.

Kawano fell to his death near Kawaguchi, in Saitama prefecture, his ramming attack in the clear blue sky having been witnessed by his brother and sister from their parents' home in Koenji, Tokyo. Kawano's victim was B-29 'Z-47' (42-24600) of the 500th BG, and it crashed to the west of Takaido Primary School, in Kugayama. Two homes were burned down and one person was killed. None of the crew survived. For his bravery, Kawano received a double rank promotion, and news of his feat reached the Emperor's ears. Kohatsu escaped with a facial wound, and for his daring he was awarded the Bukosho.

The remains of *Mrs. TITTYMOUSE* were scattered over a wide area, with the fuselage dropping in a field on the north side of Tamagawa Hospital. The tail, with the marking 'T-42', and some of the engines fell onto a barley field at Shimofuda, while eight civilians were killed in a shelter when part of the B-29's wing fell on them. Another engine came down on the railway tracks at Shibasaki. Most of the bomber crew died in the crash, and one individual who managed to take to his parachute got caught up in a tree and was subsequently killed by a mob from a nearby farming village.

Radio operator S/Sgt Norman Seliz, an identical twin whose brother Edward also served in the same group, also parachuted out. On his descent, a Japanese fighter tried to strafe him, but luckily for him, VIIth Fighter Command P-51s were on hand. A Mustang pilot waved to Seliz in a gesture of good luck, and then chased off the Japanese aircraft.

Mrs. TITTYMOUSE belonged to the 875th BS/498th BG. It was shot down into a rice field by 2Lt Satohide Kohatsu of the 244th Sentai on 7 April 1945. The bomber's nose-art was clearly visible amongst the twisted remains of the B-29, and it attracted (mostly male) onlookers from miles around (*Josh Curtis*)

JAAF 50KG AERIAL BURST BOMB

CROSS SECTION OF 50KG "TA-DAN"

0.4KG BOMB

36 X 0.4KG BOMBS IN A BREAKAWAY CANNISTER

Both the JAAF and the JNAF used aerial-burst bombs in a desperate attempt to knock down B-29s. Fighters would climb above the formation, pull ahead and then release their ordnance. Timing was critical to achieving success with this potentially devastating weapon, and only a few B-29s were ever downed with it

Seliz landed in the backyard of a house in Chofu and was captured. 'As I recall now', stated Seliz decades later, 'I appeared to be the prisoner of a particular man and woman, and they were holding my arms and dragging me through the streets. They wouldn't let anyone kill me. They beat me and kicked me, but wouldn't kill me'.

Many of the 244th Sentai crewmen went to inspect the wreckage of *MRS. TITTYMOUSE*, and while they were impressed with the 16 bomb markings indicating its completed missions, their attention was taken by the bomber's artwork – a huge nude girl painted on the nose! They crowded around chatting like serious art critics, complementing the American *esprit de corps*. Meanwhile, women looked on in disgust.

The third American casualty of the mission was B-29 42-24674 of the 499th BG, piloted by 1Lt Charles Hibbard. Damaged on its run into Tokyo by an aerial-burst bomb, the aircraft was almost certainly finished off by a 'Dinah' from the 28th Sentai. The Superfortress exploded and crashed into a field in Toyosato village, in Chiba prefecture. Eight of the crew were killed, including Hibbard. S/Sgts Arthur Gora and Ferdinand A Spacal (two of the four who parachuted) were captured, and they subsequently survived imprisonment to return home after the war.

Maj Hideo Ueda, commander of the 28th Sentai, whose 'Dinahs' went up that day, stated that his unit's aerial-burst bombs were fairly effective against B-29s. As previously mentioned, the 28th's Ki-46s were remodelled reconnaissance machines armed with 20 mm cannon and phosphorous bombs for high-altitude interception.

Despite now being classified as fighters, the 'Dinahs' pilots came from reconnaissance squadrons, and had minimal combat training. Ueda said he lost five 'Dinahs' to Mustangs on 7 April – P-51 pilots from VIIth Fighter Command claimed exactly five twin-engined fighters over Tokyo. Because of the losses, the Ki-46s were reassigned to their reconnaissance role, and Maj Ueda returned to the 'Nick'-equipped 53rd Sentai.

The 244th Sentai also fought hard on this day, but achieved little. Capt Nagao Shirai, leading the 3rd Chutai, claimed one B-29 destroyed, while WO Gannoshin Sato and Sgt Takashi Sato shared one. Capt Bunsuke

Capt Nagao Shirai was the top scorer for the 244th Sentai against the B-29s, claiming an outstanding 11 victories – he also downed two Grumman Hellcats. Shirai survived the war (*T Sakurai*)

Capt Yoshio Yoshida of the 70th Sentai poses next to his 'Tojo', which has been decorated with two B-29 victory markings. These bear the dates he claimed these victories (13 and 15 April) and his name. Yoshida had claimed six B-29s destroyed and one probable by the end of the war, and had received the Bukosho for his efforts (*Maru*)

Ikuno, leading the 1st Chutai, claimed one shot down, with another damaged, and his subordinates, 1Lt Den Ohara, 2Lt Kiyoshi Ogawa and Sgt Nihei Shindo, each inflicted damage on the enemy. In return, the death toll included Cpl Tomonobu Matsueda, who crashed into the Tama river, and 2Lt Shigeru Maeda, who came down in Obari village, in Ibaraki prefecture. Cpl Kinosuke Kihara's aircraft burst into flames when a P-51 hit him, and although his face was badly burned, he parachuted and survived.

On its tenth attempt to knock out the Musashino engine factories, the 73rd BW had finally managed it. Fine precision-bombing during clear weather led to nearly half the plant being damaged, thus breaking the curse of Target 357.

While the 73rd were busy over Tokyo, the 313th and the 314th BWs flew Mission 59 to Nagoya to try to knock out another engine plant. This was supposed to be an unescorted mission, but not completely. When a Mustang aborted 200 miles from base on the Tokyo run, 2Lt Charles C Heil of the 78th FS/15th FG jumped into his fighter on Iwo Jima to fill the void. With no navigational help, he simply pointed his P-51 in the general direction of Tokyo and 'poured on the gas'! He finally caught up with a formation of Superfortresses on their way to Nagoya. Undaunted, he took on the huge task of guarding all 153 B-29s.

2Lt Kaoru Tsujimoto of the 5th
Sentai rammed Capt Frank
Crowcroft's B-29 over Ise Bay,
Nagoya, on 7 April 1945. All but
three of the B-29 crewmen died.
Both Tsujimoto and his observer,
Cpl Masayuki Kato, also perished
(*Y Kumoi*)

RAMBLIN ROSCOE of the 882nd BS/
500th BG had two of its engines shot
out by fighters over Tokyo on the
night of 13 April 1945. It still made it
back to Saipan, however, where its
pilot crash-landed and struck a truck,
before coming to rest on this
embankment (*Josh Curtis*)

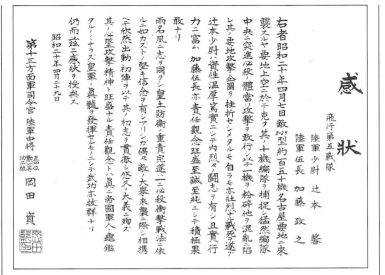

The posthumous citation issued to 2Lt Karou Tsujimoto and his observer, Cpl Masayuki Kato. It reads;

'For heroic and outstanding services in connection with the interception of about 150 enemy B-29s engaged over the Nagoya area on 7 April 1945 – the aforementioned flyers caught a ten-aircraft formation. Flying into the centre of this formation, they destoyed a B-29 by ramming, and also plunged the other bombers into confusion, thus forcing them to fail in their intended attacks on targets. Both 2Lt Tsujimoto and Cpl Kato died heroic deaths in action. 2Lt Tsujimoto was a person of action, with a gentle and sincere character, full of fighting spirit. Cpl Kato was a purely faithful and brave person, with a strong sense of responsibility. While both had firmly believed that there would be no other way to down the B-29s other than by employing ramming tactics, and thus complete their duty to defend the soil of the Empire, they did not baulk in taking off when the enemy arrived in great strength. They carried out their original intentions, and sacrificed themselves for the great cause. Their spirit of attack, both in respect to the kill itself and their sense of responsibility, is a model of the Imperial military men, and their conduct exhibited the soul and essence of the Imperial Army. Signed, Lt Gen Tasuku Okada, Commander of the 13th Area Army, 29 April 1945'

Flying B-29 42-65350 was Capt Frank Crowcroft of the 29th BG, whose wife had recently given birth to a baby girl. On a previous mission, a news reporter had accompanied Crowcroft's crew on a bombing mission over Japan. The correspondent had later described in chilling detail an attempted ramming by a twin-engined aircraft. The reporter had also interviewed Crowcroft's wife and relatives of the other crew members for a radio broadcast, and they had been delighted to hear about the lucky escape. But soon after the broadcast the crew's luck was to change.

At Kiyosu airfield, south-east of Nagoya, 2Lt Kaoru Tsujimoto of the 5th Sentai received his orders to scramble, and he took off in his 'Nick'. Over Ise Bay, he and his observer Cpl Masayuki Kato rammed their twin-engined fighter into Crowcroft's B-29.

The bomber's flight engineer, Sgt Melvin L Greene, remembered how the collision opened up a hole in the fuselage next to him, and he bailed out. The navigator also exited, but his 'chute did not fully open and he was killed. The two waist gunners parachuted into captivity and survived the war. The rest of the crew perished.

Unlike the Tokyo raid, the mission to Nagoya attracted a meagre fighter response. Bomber gunners claimed 21 destroyed, 11 probables and 22 damaged, and two Superfortresses were lost. Not to be outdone by the 73rd, the bombardiers of the 313th and 314th BWs hit and damaged 94 per cent of their targets in the Nagoya area, destroying more than 200 machine tools. The target factory never recovered.

The 73rd BW lost three bombers over Tokyo, while the combined 313th/314th BW raid on Nagoya cost two. The JAAF had scrambled 119 fighters, and their overall claims on the day were 14 destroyed and 40 damaged, for the loss of 16 fighters and five heavily damaged. The Mustangs claimed 21 victories for the loss of two of their own, while the Superfortress gunners believed they had shot down 80 Japanese fighters!

The first long-range P-51 escort mission over Japan marked the beginning of the end for Japanese fighters in home defence, for twin-engined interceptors would no longer be able to make daylight attacks, and single-engined losses would start to rise dramatically.

FINAL PHASE AGAINST THE B-29

The invasion of Okinawa began on 1 April 1945, when US warships bombarded the island prior to more than 60,000 troops being put ashore. Some Japanese believed the fall of Saipan had sealed their fate, while many others thought the loss of Okinawa would surely do so. Under immense pressure, the Japanese Navy and Army finally co-operated in launching a series of *kamikaze* suicide attacks against Allied ships supporting the Okinawan campaign.

Adm Chester Nimitz wanted the *kamikaze* bases in Kyushu neutralised, and Gen LeMay received his orders to destroy their staging areas. The head of XXI Bomber Command reluctantly accepted this directive, although he believed that using B-29s for the tactical bombing of airfields would achieve limited results. Each unit was assigned to hit a specific airfield, and the bombers encountered little opposition compared with the heavy flak and fighter defences they had endured over industrial targets.

Northern Kyushu was in the home defence zone of the JAAF's 4th Sentai, based at Ozuki airfield in western Honshu. The 4th was the only Army group of any significant size in the area, and it had experience of fighting B-29s. The unit's only weapon was the twin-engined Ki-45 'Nick'.

An airfield in Kyushu is seen under attack in April 1945. *Kamikaze* **missions from numerous bases in southern Kyushu posed a tremendous threat to US naval forces off Okinawa. In order to render these sites inoperable for as long as possible, the B-29s dropped both fragmentation and time-delayed bombs (*US Navy*)**

Despite possessing a range of over 1400 miles, the Ki-45s of the 4th Sentai were hard pressed to reach southern Kyushu, where most of the *kamikaze* bases were located, due to the fact that the unit already had its hands full protecting northern Kyushu. To solve this problem, the JAAF's 56th Sentai was temporarily relocated from Itami to Ashiya, in Fukuoka prefecture, in March, and it remained here supporting the air defence effort through to May. However, the combat radius of this unit was limited to northern and eastern Kyushu, which lacked anti-bomber fighter cover. The 56th was exclusively armed with the 'Tony'.

The protection of the Kyushu bases ultimately fell on the Navy, which had little experience of tackling B-29s. It had previously been discovered that the standard Zero fighter was generally ineffective against the Super-fortress, and although the 343rd Kokutai, operating from Kanoya and Kokubu airfields, had commenced the defence of Kyushu with the all-new Kawanishi N1K2 *Shiden-Kai* 'George', these too proved unsuited to bomber interception. The crews of the Army's 4th Sentai were old hands in fighting the Superfortresses, but the pilots of the 343rd were not. Indeed, their mission up to now had been to support the Okinawan *kamikaze* operations by intercepting American carrier fighters.

The 343rd's 'George' fighters could do little to stop the B-29s roaming over Kyushu at will, so in an effort to at least stop the bombers venturing over southern Kyushu, 'Jack' fighters from the 302nd Kokutai (which had previously engaged B-29s) at Atsugi were transferred down to Kanoya in April and May. In addition, 'Jacks' from the 332nd (in Naruo) and the 352nd (in Omura) Kokutai were gathered at Kanoya.

The first B-29 bombing mission in support of the Okinawan landings took place on 8 April, when the 73rd BW were scheduled to bomb Kanoya. The typically uncooperative Japanese weather clouded over the target, however, and the Superfortresses were forced to bomb Kagoshima by radar. There was no fighter opposition, and no B-29s were lost. On the same day, the 73rd and 313th BWs joined forces on Missions No 60 and 61 and dropped 192 tons of bombs on various Kyushu airfields – only one B-29 was brought down.

Capt Yoshio Yoshida's 70th Sentai Ki-44-II-Hei is seen sporting six victory markings at Kashiwa airfield, near Tokyo, in June 1945. Its pilot scored his last victory (at night) on 25 May 1945 over the capital. XXI Bomber Command lost no less than 26 B-29s to all causes on this day – a record figure that was never exceeded (*Y Izawa*)

Regularly during the month of April, the 4th Sentai sent up its 'Nicks' against the bomber streams, and lost three pilots in ramming attacks. For example, on 17 April the 73rd, 313th and 314th BWs flew a combined total of six missions, with 118 aircraft bombing various airfields. The 4th opposed these raids, and Sgt Tsutomu Nishimura reportedly rammed a B-29 – none were lost, however.

The following day, 112 B-29s came back to finish off the airfields. This time Maj Furukawa led his 56th Sentai 'Tonys' into the fray from Ashiya, intercepting the B-29s over Tachiarai airfield. The fighters swarmed over the bombers, and the 497th BG endured a beating. *Coral Queen* (42-24615) took hits in the left wing and tail, and began losing fuel – it would eventually ditch near Iwo Jima, and only three crew were rescued. *Texas Doll* (42-24627) took 350 hits, but amazingly none of the crew was injured and the aircraft made it home.

Sgt Chikao Yoshino (Maj Furukawa's wingman) hit a B-29 during a head-on attack after his CO had completed his pass, but the bomber's gunners hit back. Yoshino tried to make an emergency landing at Tachiarai airfield, which had been left potholed and battered by the B-29s, but his 'Tony' hit a crater and he was thrown out of the cockpit when the aircraft nosed over. He died a few days later in hospital. Maj Furukawa credited his wingman with a probable B-29 kill.

On 18 April 1945, 2Lt Miosaburo Yamamoto of the 4th Sentai was hit when he made his run into a formation of B-29s. With his Ki-45 on fire and smoking badly, he continued his dive into a second formation of bombers and slammed into the right wing of *Gonna Mak'er,* piloted by 1Lt Robert J Anderson. All were killed (*M Kobayashi*)

Meanwhile, *Gonna Mak'er* (42-65231) was flying on borrowed time. 2Lt Miosaburo Yamamoto, leader of the 4th Sentai's ramming section, flew his 'Nick' through the 497th formation and slammed directly into it. Lt Ed Cutler, pilot of *Texas Doll*, saw the sickening impact, and recalled;

'I watched, spellbound, as the tail and right wing (almost all 123 ft of it) came off, and the No 4 engine broke loose and climbed majestically straight up – all by itself, still running.'

Two B-29s had been lost on the raid, but the Americans had been able to drop 436 tons of bombs on various airfields. The crews reported that both fighter opposition and flak were weak. Adm Matome Ugaki, in charge of *kamikaze* operations, was incensed that the bombing raids had delayed his sorties, which were further hampered long after the B-29s had departed by the detonation of fragmentation and time-delayed bombs on his airfields.

The 7 May mission to the Kyushu airfields proved a sobering experience for the 505th BG. In the last phase of the anti-*kamikaze* effort, the 313th BW succeeded in getting 41 Superfortresses over the primary targets, which dropped 238 tons of high explosives on Oita, Usa, Ibusuki and Kanoya airfields. The bombers went in unescorted, giving the 'Nicks' the freedom to act. Three aircraft from the 505th were scythed down.

The ramming unit of the 4th Sentai. M/Sgt Tsutomu Murata, sitting on the right, rammed *Empire Express* on 7 May 1945 and was killed. Note the flags on each crewman's sleeve (as well as the ramming artwork on the nose of the Ki-45 parked behind them). In February 1945, a critically burned Japanese pilot parachuted to earth, and unable to speak, he was beaten to death by a mob who mistook him for an American. To prevent the recurrence of such a tragedy, the military ordered all pilots to sew flags onto their flying suits (*via H Sakaida*)

2Lt Hannoshin Nishio stands by his 'Nick' in June 1945. By the time this photograph was taken the veteran fighter pilot had already claimed five B-29s destroyed. The inscription on the fuselage of his Ki-45 indicates that this machine was a presentation aircraft paid for by private subscription, and then donated to the JAAF for frontline service (*H Nishio*)

The first to fall was 1Lt James McKillip's *Empire Express* (42-63549), which was rammed by MSgt Tsutomu Murata of the 4th Sentai shortly after its bombs had fallen over Usa airfield. The Ki-45 was hit and on fire when it flew into the B-29, which quickly disintegrated and fell together with Murata's aircraft. The wreckage came down at the foot of Mt Hachimen, in Oita prefecture. After the war, the families of the downed B-29 crewmen erected a monument near the crash site. A map of America was engraved on the stone monument, the former featuring inlaid stones from each crewmans' home state. A memorial to Murata was also erected.

His colleague, Sgt Ryoichi Kaneko, was also killed in a ramming attack on this day, but the circumstances remain unknown.

The last known aerial ramming attacks by JAAF fighters took place on 26 June 1945, when XXI Bomber Command sent 426 B-29s on nine missions over Central Honshu, hitting aircraft factories at Nagoya, Osaka and other nearby industrial cities. Fighter opposition at this late stage in the war was extremely poor, mostly due to shortages of both fuel and experienced pilots. And if the JAAF did venture aloft, aggressive fighter

escorts usually prevented them from reaching the B-29s. Despite these factors, 24 'Franks' and 'Tojos' of the 246th Sentai, led by Maj Kanshi Ishikawa, took off from Taisho to effect an interception.

Over Kumano Nada, 1st Chutai leader Capt Sadahiko Otonari, and his wingman Sgt Minoru Hara, attacked a formation of 12 B-29s – the pair reportedly rammed their fighters into B-29s and were killed. Otonari's final record was four B-29s destroyed and eight damaged. The 246th Sentai claimed six B-29s in the day's action for the loss of three pilots.

The Kawasaki aircraft factory at Kagamigahara, north of Nagoya, was the primary target for the 19th BG on this day. Leading the formation was the *City of Chicago* (42-94003) from the 28th BS, piloted by Capt Van R Parker. The mission started to go wrong at the rendezvous point off the Japanese coast, where limited visibility due to heavy cloud cover caused problems for the pilots as they tried to get their formations together. Japanese fighters came out to meet them, quickly shooting a bomber down, and forcing 1Lt Hans Gammel to abort in order to help rescue the downed crewmen (who were eventually saved by a submarine). Capt Benjamin G Kordus, who had seen heavy action in Europe in B-17s, assumed Gammel's position in the formation.

The 19th proceeded to the target, picking up aircraft from other squadrons which had also been unable to get into formation. As they crossed the shoreline, the clouds began breaking up.

Although the improved visibility helped the B-29s assume a defensive formation, as well as navigate to the target, these conditions also aided the Japanese fighters as they positioned themselves for an attack. The 56th Sentai's 2Lt Yutaka Nakagawa, and his wingman, came into contact with

The smouldering wreckage of a B-29 downed in Fuse, east Osaka, in May 1945. B-29 crashes in residential areas caused massive destruction and loss of life due to the all-wooden construction of most Japanese homes (*Y Kumoi*)

the 19th BG over Hakusan, in Mie prefecture, as the huge formation flew towards Lake Biwa. The two 'Tony' pilots made a frontal assault, and were met with a blistering shower of lead. With his aircraft trailing smoke, Nakagawa flew straight into Capt Parker's path.

'Our ship was vibrating with the noise and recoil of our 0.50-calibre guns', Parker remembered. 'Still the Jap kept coming. Why didn't he blow up, disintegrating like so many others I had seen after encountering our curtain of lead? But no, he kept boring in, straight for the nose of our plane. I thought to myself, "So this is it. This is how it's going to end", and I braced for the impact that would snuff out my life, and the lives of my crew members'.

Nakagawa passed over the right wing of Parker's B-29 and slammed into 44-69873. Parker heard his central fire control gunner yell out, 'My God! He got Kordus!' According to eyewitnesses, the rammed B-29 had its right wing knocked off. The 'Tony' broke apart in the air and the pilot was ejected from the cockpit. S/Sgt Lester J Shelters, the B-29's tail gunner, was the only crewman to bail out. He was taken into custody by military police and sent on to Tokai Army HQ. Shelters was executed in July 1945 in Nagoya.

Nakagawa, whose torso was cut in half, came down by parachute and his body was discovered hanging in a pine tree in front of the main building in the compound of the Shinkoji Temple in Hisai, near the west coast of Ise Bay.

After 26 June, Japanese fighters were rarely encountered in numbers – the sky now belonged to the B-29s, and they ranged at will. The JAAF was virtually powerless to react against the invaders, and it was told to keep its remaining aircraft in reserve for the final battle, expected in the autumn.

The moment of impact. 2Lt Yutaka Nakagawa rams the B-29 of Capt Benjamin Kordus over Hakusan on 26 June 1945. This was the last reported ramming by a JAAF pilot during the war

2Lt Yutaka Nakagawa of the Ki-61-equipped 56th Sentai (*Y Kumoi*)

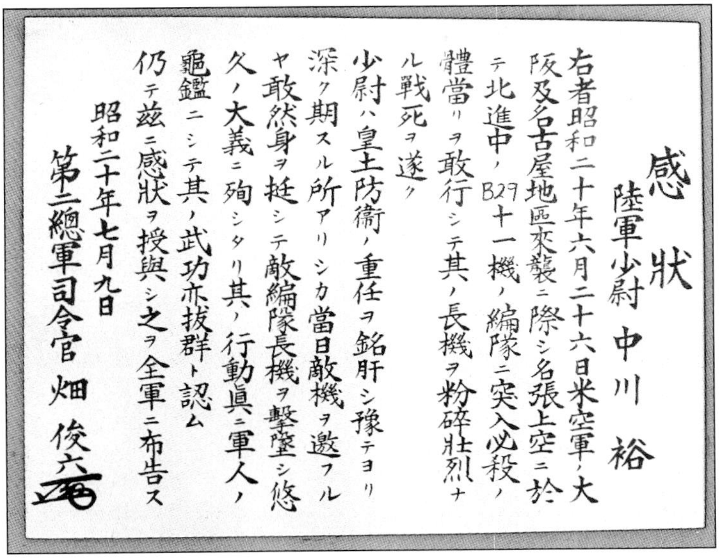

The posthumous citation to 2Lt Yutaka Nakagawa for his ramming attack of 26 June 1945. It reads in part;

'For heroic and outstanding services in connection with the interception of USAAF aircraft strikes on the Osaka and Nagoya areas on 26 June 1945, the aforementioned pilot went into an 11-aircraft formation of B-29s heading north over Nabari and broke the lead aircraft into pieces by ramming, dying a heroic death in action. While 2Lt Nakagawa had fully realised his grave duty to guard the soil of the Empire, and was deeply determined to carry out his duty, he bravely dared to ram the enemy lead aircraft when he met them, sacrificing himself in the great cause. His action is truly a model of the military men, and his services are recognised to be outstanding. Signed, Gen Shunroku Hata, 2nd General Army, dated 9 July 1945'

感　狀

陸軍少尉　中川　裕

右者昭和二十年六月二十六日米空軍ノ大阪及ビ名古屋地區來襲ニ際シ名張上空ニ於テ北進中ノ B29 十一機ノ編隊ニ突入必殺ニ體當リヲ敢行シテ其ノ長機ヲ粉碎壯烈ナル戰死ヲ遂ノ

少尉ハ皇土防衛ノ重任ヲ銘肝シ豫テリ深ク期スル所アリシカ當日敵機ヲ邀フルヤ敢然身ヲ挺シテ敵編隊長機ヲ撃墜シ悠久ノ大義ニ殉シタリ其ノ行動眞ニ軍人ノ龜鑑ニシテ其ノ武功亦拔群ト認ム

仍テ茲ニ感狀ヲ授與シ之ヲ全軍ニ布告ス

昭和二十年七月九日
第二總軍司令官　畑　俊六

Japan's industrial power had been weakened, and the means to defend its airspace was lacking. In addition to a shortage of aircraft and trained pilots, there was a scarcity of radio equipment and searchlights. Although the Superfortress suffered losses on missions right up to the end of the war, these were mainly due to operational reasons, or through anti-aircraft fire.

JAPANESE LOSSES IN THE B-29 CAMPAIGN

The statistics on overall Japanese losses in B-29 bombing raids are many and varied. One source cites 241,309 people killed, 213,041 injured and 2,333,388 homes destroyed. No one really knows the true numbers, for many public buildings that housed such information were destroyed during the raids themselves.

But no matter what the real figures are, it is a fact that a tremendous number of people perished. War orphans flooded into the streets of Tokyo and other large cities, and most citizens were directly or indirectly affected by the huge destruction. By the time Japan surrendered, its economy was in ruins.

Five of Japan's great cities – Tokyo, Osaka, Kobe, Nagoya and Yokohama –- had been totally destroyed. In addition, the two smaller cities of Hiroshima and Nagasaki were erased from the face of the earth in the atomic bombing. The major industrial centres were wrecked, and inaccurate bombing had destroyed or damaged many smaller cities and towns.

Typical of the conflagration brought about through massive fire-bombing, the city of Toyama goes up in flames on the night of 2 August 1945. No B-29s were lost on this mission. XXI Bomber Command continued to hit targets right up until the Japanese surrendered on 15 August 1945 (*Josh Curtis*)

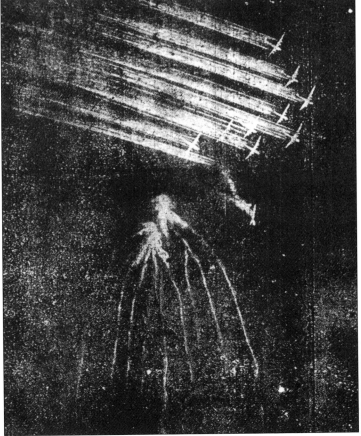

In this dramatic shot, taken on 1 June 1945 over Osaka by B-29 crewman Chester Marshall, Capt Wilkerson's *Abroad With Eleven Yanks* (from the 877th BS/499th BG) is shown nose-up just below the port inner engine of Superfortress 'V-45'. Already starting to spin in, the bomber had suffered a direct hit by flak and all hands were lost (*Josh Curtis*)

This newspaper photograph shows *Abroad With Eleven Yanks* falling out of the sky over Osaka (*Y Kumoi*)

The Allied forces, fighting on many fronts, had turned the tide against the Japanese and ground them down, helped in no small part by the B-29, a 'high-tech' product of American science and industrial might. While many factors contributed to forcing their surrender, the Japanese people believed they were ultimately defeated by the Boeing B-29 Superfortress.

THE FATE OF CAPTURED B-29 CREWS

Japan was a model in treating PoWs in the Russo-Japanese War of 1905 and World War 1 (Japan was partly involved in World War 1, and had taken German prisoners). The Japanese observed international codes and

This was how the port of Osaka appeared from 19,200 ft after the B-29s had dropped their load on 1 June 1945. Flak and fighter attacks were fierce on this day, and ten Superfortresses failed to return (*Josh Curtis*)

practices. However, the country's attitude towards the treatment of PoWs changed drastically during World War 2.

The government and military leaders made little effort to inform their soldiers and citizens about the Geneva Convention. And although the Japanese government announced at the beginning of the Pacific War that the rules of the Geneva Convention would be respected and applied to all prisoners, this edict was never officially ratified.

Instead, Premier Hideki Tojo issued a directive called the Field Service Code to the military in the first months of the war. It stated that to be captured in combat was a disgrace. This doctrine was constantly reinforced, from training to the battlefield, resulting in Japanese forces fighting virtually to annihilation. Enemy soldiers who were captured were treated with even greater contempt.

The inhumane and brutal treatment of prisoners stems from the way the Japanese military treated its own men. It did not respect the lives of its own soldiers as a whole, the military instead being a strict and abusive institution. Beatings of young trainees for the slightest infraction was a part of their training. Physical and verbal abuse, and fear of their NCOs, turned young soldiers into mechanical robots that carried out orders without question. Robbed of any compassion and empathy, and filled with anger and hatred of the deplorable war situation, they took revenge on helpless prisoners.

The Japanese army's military police (*Kempei Tai*) were notorious for their brutal interrogations of captured B-29 crews. Even their own citizens

The remains of B-29 44-70008 of the 525th BS/29th BG came to rest in a rice field in Kobe on 5 June 1945, having fallen victim to flak (*Y Kumoi*)

disliked and feared them. The interrogators had no concept of western psychology and values, and they resorted to the crudest of methods – torture. The information extracted from crewmen under these sadistic circumstances was of little value.

Kyoto historian Toru Fukubayashi recently carried out a lengthy and meticulous investigation of B-29 crash sites, and the fate of the crews. His research is based on documents from the General Headquarters (GHQ) of the Allied Forces, testimonies taken from the War Crimes Trial held in Yokohama, Japanese witnesses and the Missing Air Crew Reports (MACRs). He has obtained the following figures.

Approximately 545 Allied flyers, including B-29 crews, were captured on the Japanese homeland including the Nansei Islands, but excluding the Chishima (Kuriles) and Bonin Islands. Of this total, 29 individuals (including one Britain) were found dead or were killed at the time of capture, including deaths on transit from the place of capture to the *Kempei Tai*. Ninety-four died from injuries, disease, medical neglect or accidents in confinement – 52 of these individuals perished in a blaze that gutted the Tokyo Army Prison during a B-29 fire raid on 26 May 1945, and 11 were killed at the Chugoku *Kempei Tai* HQ on 6 August 1945 by the atomic bomb dropped on Hiroshima. A further 132 were executed, and 290 (including seven Englishmen) were liberated from PoW camps. The rate of return for all Allied PoWs in Japan was 53 per cent.

The identity of this B-29 seen plunging to its death over Kobe on 5 June 1945 remains unknown (*Y Kumoi*)

Senior members of the Japanese war cabinet issued two secret notices to the military in respect to the treatment of captured airmen. The first was issued in the name of the Army Vice-Minister as of 28 July 1942 in the aftermath of the Doolittle Raid. It stated that violators of the International War Code would be treated as war criminals, while those who did not violate the provisions were to be treated as prisoners of war. The second notice, dated 8 September 1944, stated that indiscriminate bombing constituted a war crime punishable by execution.

Treatment of prisoners differed among military administrative districts. In Tokai (Nagoya as the main city), Chubu (Kinki and Osaka) and Seibu (Kyushu and Fukuoka), B-29 crewmen were sometimes given a quick and illegal military trial, then condemned to death, with the

Maj Haruyoshi Furukawa, commander of the 56th Sentai in 1944-45, stands beside the monument at Chokoji Temple, near Itami airfield, that is dedicated to the pilots from his unit who were killed in action. The 56th claimed 11 B-29s shot down for the loss of 30 pilots. This photograph was taken on 24 October 1998 (*K Takaki*)

sentence quickly administered. Others were arbitrarily executed by the military police. In Tobu district (Tokyo area) and elsewhere, there were no organised executions. Therefore, B-29 crews dropping down in Nagoya or Kobe were more likely to be executed than those who were captured around Tokyo.

Many trials of B- and C-class war criminals held in Yokohama after the war related to the mistreatment and arbitrary executions of B-29 crews. Most of the high-ranking officers who ran the prison camps, as well as the guards, were tried and convicted. Those who were not executed received prison sentences of varying severity.

The Japan-US Peace Treaty was signed in 1949, and the following year the Korean War began. The United States began releasing war criminals in a gesture of political goodwill following the start of the war, and then handed over responsibility for the rest to the Japanese government. However, not all the convicts were released during this period. For instance, one prisoner who was sentenced to 25 years' hard labour was not freed until 1957.

The release of war criminals was a politically-motivated move made by the US government at a time when it needed Japan's support during the new conflict, as well as a partner against the growing menace of the Soviet Union and Communist Red China in Asia.

This B-29 memorial was dedicated at the USAF Academy in Colorado Springs, Colorado, in September 2000. It pays tribute to the men and women who built the aircraft, the mechanics who serviced it and the crews who took it into action (*Hap Halloran*)

APPENDICES

APPENDIX 1

B-29 LOSSES (including operational losses on combat missions)

	Date	Target	Lost
XX BC (58th BW)	15-16 June 1944 to 6 January 1945	Yawata, Omura	38
	7 July to 21 December 1944	Manchuria	18
			Total - 56
XXI BC	24 November 1944 to 27 January 1945	Areas including Tokyo	50
	27-31 March 1945	Tachiarai airfield	1
	27 March to 8 August 1945	Mining missions	9
	4-25 February 1945	Areas including Tokyo	24
	4-31 March 1945	Areas including Tokyo	27
	1-30 April 1945	Areas including Tokyo	39
	8 April to 11 May 1945	Kyushu airfields	23
	10 May to 30 June 1945	Areas including Tokyo	98
	1 July to 15 August 1945	Local cities	33
			Total - 304

OVERALL TOTAL LOSSES - 360

APPENDIX 2

TOP B-29 HUNTERS OF THE JAAF

Listed in this appendix are the names of the pilots who claimed, or were attributed with, B-29 victories. In most cases, it was almost impossible for any individual pilot to single-handedly destroy a Superfortress. Often, pilots claimed a victory if the bomber emitted smoke and fell out of formation, thinking it would not survive. It is believed that many pilots were over-optimistic in claiming victories, and this is backed up by each sides' records for specific missions. In almost all cases, the claims for kills far exceeded the number of actual losses.

Pilot	Unit	B-29 claims	Remarks
Capt Fujitaro Ito*	5th Sentai	17	20 B-29s damaged
Capt Nagao Shirai	244th Sentai	11	Plus one F6Fs
Capt Chuichi Ichikawa*	244th Sentai	9	Plus one F6F
Capt Kensui Kono	70th Sentai	9	KIA
2Lt Sadamitsu Kimura*	4th Sentai	8	KIA
Capt Isamu Kashiide*	4th Sentai	7	7 kills at Nomonhan
2Lt Makoto Ogawa*	70th Sentai	7	Plus two P-51Ds
Capt Yoshio Yoshida*	70th Sentai	6	
Sgt Nobuji Negishi*	53rd Sentai	6	
WO Isamu Sasaki*	Test Centre Fighter Unit	6	38 kills in total
T/Sgt Moriyoshi Torizuka*	53rd Sentai	6	
WO Hannoshin Nishio	4th Sentai	5	
WO Tadao Sumi*	56th Sentai	5	Plus one P-51
WO Akira Kawakita	9th Sentai	5	KIA 1944
Capt Junichi Ogata	56th Sentai	4	KIA ramming
Capt Sadahiko Otonari	246th Sentai	4	KIA ramming
M/Sgt Isamu Hotani*	5th Sentai	4	
Capt Mitsuo Oyake*	18th Sentai	4	Rammed, survived
Capt Haruo Kitamura	18th Sentai	4	Rammed, survived
2Lt Takeo Adachi	55th Sentai	4	KIA
Maj Masaji Kobayashi	4th Sentai	4	
1/Lt Minoru Shirota	55th Sentai	4	KIA
1/Lt Heikichi Yoshizawa	47th Sentai	4	KIA ramming
M/Sgt Minoru Uchida	4th Sentai	3	
M/Sgt Tatsuo Morimoto	4th Sentai	3	KIA
Capt Toshio Sassa	4th Sentai	3	
Sgt Shintaro Fujimoto	4th Sentai	3	
Sgt Tomokitsu Yamada	23rd Sentai	3	
M/Sgt Kenji Fujimoto*	246th Sentai	3	Survived two rammings
Maj Yasuhiko Kuroe	Test Centre Fighter Unit	3	30 kills in total
Maj Atsuyuki Sakato	70th Sentai	3	
T/Sgt Akio Nakagaki	53rd Sentai	3	
T/Sgt Kiyoshi Otaki	70th Sentai	3	
1Lt Naoyuki Ogata*	59th Sentai	3	Plus one F6F and one P-51
WO Yoshio Sakaguchi*	5th Sentai	3	
Sgt Matsumi Nakano*	244th Sentai	3	Plus two F6Fs
Maj Teruhiko Kobayashi*	244th Sentai	3	Plus two F6Fs

* – Bukosho recipient

APPENDIX 3

B-29 MISSIONS SUBJECTED TO JAAF RAMMING ATTACKS

	Mission	Date	Target	Wing(s)	B-29s up	Lost
XX BOMBER COMMAND	7	20 Aug 1944	Yawata	58	88	14
	19	7 Dec 1944	Mukden	58	108	7
	23	21 Dec 1944	Mukden	58	49	2
XXI BOMBER COMMAND	7	24 Nov 1944	Tokyo	73	111	2
	10	3 Dec 1944	Tokyo	73	86	5
	12	13 Dec 1944	Nagoya	73	90	4
	13	18 Dec 1944	Nagoya	73	89	4
	14	22 Dec 1944	Nagoya	73	78	3
	16	27 Dec 1944	Tokyo	73	72	3
	17	3 Jan 1945	Nagoya	73	97	5
	18	9 Jan 1945	Tokyo	73	72	6
	24	27 Jan 1945	Tokyo	73	76	9
	29	10 Feb 1945	Ota	73/313	118	12
	37	19 Feb 1945	Tokyo	73/313	150	6
	34	15 Mar 1945	Nagoya	73/313	117	1
	43	16-17 Mar 1945	Kobe	73/313/314	330	3
	58	7 Apr 1945	Tokyo	73	107	3
	59	7 Apr 1945	Nagoya	313/314	194	2
	70-75	17 Apr 1945	Kyushu	73/313/314	118	0
	76-81	18 Apr 1945	Kyushu	73/313/314	112	2
	151-54	7 May 1945	Kyushu	313	41	3
	186	29 May 1945	Yokohama	73/313/314	454	7
	189	7 June 1945	Osaka	73/313/314	409	2
	223-31	26 June 1945	Osaka/Nagoya	58/73/313/314	426	6

COLOUR PLATES

1

Ki-44-II-Otsu of the 3rd Chutai/47th Sentai, Chofu airfield, October 1944

Known by the Allied code-name of 'Tojo', the Ki-44 was the fastest-climbing fighter in the JAAF's arsenal. The *Shoki* ('Devil Queller') flew like a truck when compared with the lighter Ki-43 'Oscar' and the Ki-61 'Tony', but was extremely rugged and quite suited for attacking B-29s. It was often misidentified as the American P-47 Thunderbolt or the JNAF's 'Jack' fighter due to its large radial engine and stubby appearance. This particular model sported two 12.7 mm machine guns in the nose and one 20 mm cannon in each wing, and boasted a reflector gunsight – others had the simpler tube sight.

2

Ki-61-I-Hei of the 2nd Chutai/244th Sentai, flown by M/Sgt Tadao Sumi, Chofu airfield, November 1944

The pilot of this particular Ki-61, Tadao Sumi, was born in 1916 in Gifu Prefecture. He joined the army in the mid-1930s, and had seen service as an infantryman during the sieges of Shanghai and Nanking, prior to transferring to flight training in February 1941. Sumi graduated in November of that year, and was eventually assigned to the air defence of the Tokyo region with the 244th Sentai when it formed in the aftermath of the Doolittle Raid in April 1942.

It was not until Sumi started flying against B-29s towards the end of 1944 that he became a hero in the eyes of the Japanese public. Having joined the Ki-61-equipped 56th Sentai just prior to the first raids, he subsequently fought the B-29s on a near-daily basis until war's end.

Sumi's greatest moment came during a series of night actions fought on 13 March 1945 over Osaka, the master sergeant making repeated lone attacks on the B-29 force. He succeeded in shooting down four bombers, and damaging three others, before he was forced to take to his parachute when his Ki-61 ran out of fuel. However, as he undid his straps and prepared to vacate his fighter, Sumi became disoriented through an attack of vertigo. This momentarily delayed his jump to the point that when he did part company with the Ki-61, he struck his shoulder on the tailplane as the aircraft flew on. Sumi was forced to spend three months in hospital recuperating.

In recognition of his heroic deed, Gen Kawabe, commander of the 15th Military District, promoted Sumi to warrant officer and presented him with a letter of commendation. On 21 June 1945, Sumi also received the Bukosho (Medal of Honour, A Class – he was one of the very few recipients to receive the highest grade of this decoration). He went back into combat later that month, and despite being wounded again, continued to fly. By war's end Sumi had downed five B-29s and damaged four more, and had also been credited with destroying a P-51D. He passed away on 25 July 1985.

3

Ki-45-KAI of the 3rd Chutai/53rd Sentai, flown by Sgt Nobuji Negishi, Matsudo airfield, November 1944

Nobuji Negishi became the top B-29 hunter of the 53rd Sentai during the home defence period. He was born in 1924 in Saitama Prefecture, and entered the Tokyo Army Aviation School in October 1939. Upon graduation in 1942, Negishi was assigned to the 244th Sentai, which had just been formed to guard the capital.

A short while later he transferred to the 18th Sentai, before moving again to the 53rd – both units were Japan-based. The latter sentai had been formed specifically with Ki-45s so as to counter the B-29 forays over Japan, and the unit marked all of its 'Nicks' with a stylised number 53 on the large vertical surface. Sgt Negishi's first night mission on 10 March 1945 yielded instant success, for when ground searchlights lit up a formation of Superfortresses, he succeeded in knocking down two with precision shooting. On 9 July 1945 Negishi was decorated with the award of the Bukosho for his successful missions against the B-29s. He ended the war with six Superfortress kills, and had damaged a further seven bombers.

4

Ki-44-II-Otsu of the 47th Sentai Shinten *Seiku* Tai, flown by M/Sgt Isamu Sakamoto, Narimasu airfield, late 1944

Shinten ('Quaking the Heavens') Special Attack sections were formed within the home defence units based around Tokyo under 10th Fighter Division control. Their mission was air-to-air ramming of B-29s, and the red tail on this particular Ki-44 indicates that aircraft No 32 was a special attack fighter. The 'Tojo' could climb to 5000 m (16,405 ft) in a little over four minutes, and had a service ceiling of 11,200 m (36,745 ft) under test conditions. However, in combat its performance was considerably reduced when flying with a full load of fuel and ammunition.

5

Ki-46-III-KAI of the 16th Independent Chutai, Taisho airfield, December 1944

This 'Dinah' sports the *Kikusui* (floating chrysanthemum) emblem on its tail, which symbolised loyalty to the Emperor – this marking was not a *kamikaze* emblem, although many suicide units used it. The 73rd BW specifically targeted the Mitsubishi factory at Nagoya that produced this high-altitude reconnaissance aeroplane. Based at Taisho airfield, in Osaka, the 16th Independent Chutai was a part of the 18th Fighter Division. The Ki-46-III was capable of speeds up to 630 kmh (391 mph) at 6000 m (19,685 ft), and it had a service ceiling of 10,500 m (34,450 ft). Although the Ki-46-III-KAI variant carried no weapons, it nevertheless played a crucial role in the interception of B-29s by detecting approaching bombers during dedicated high-altitude patrols over the home islands.

6

Ki-46-III-KAI of the 17th Independent Chutai, Chofu airfield, December 1944

The 17th Independent Chutai belonged to the 10th Fighter Division, which provided protection for the Imperial capital. Although the unit was equipped with the fastest operational twin-engined reconnaissance aircraft in service with the JAAF, its Ki-46s were not well suited for intercepting B-29s because of their slow climbing speed – it took a little over 20 minutes to reach 8000 m (26,250 ft)! This particular aircraft has been modified to carry two

20 mm Ho-5 cannon in the nose, and a 37 mm Ho-203 cannon mounted obliquely behind the pilot and observer. The Ki-46-III-KAI enjoyed little success against the B-29.

7

Ki-46-III-KAI of the 28th Sentai, flown by T/Sgt Etsuo Kitagawa, Togane airfield, December 1944
On 27 December 1944 T/Sgt Etsuo Kitagawa used this aircraft to claim one B-29 shot down (unconfirmed) and a further two damaged. His aircraft was in turn hit in the left fuel tank by defensive fire from one of the bombers, and he was forced to land at Togane airfield. After the mission, one yellow (victory) and two white stars (damaged) were painted on the rear fuselage to record the pilot's credits. The unit insignia on the rudder took the form of a red sun surrounded by white, while the two horizontal bars indicated that this aircraft belonged to the 2nd Squadron.

8

Ki-45-KAI-Ko of the 2nd Chutai/4th Sentai, flown by Lt Isamu Kashiide, Kozuki airfield, late 1944
Isamu Kashiide used this machine to perfect his lethal method of head-on attacks against B-29s over Japan in 1944-45. He enjoyed considerable success with this technique, claiming to have downed some 26 Superfortresses. Kashiide's 'Nick' boasted a 37 mm cannon as its primary weapon, his observer's hand-held single 7.92 mm machine-gun proving next to useless in fending off P-51D and P-47N escort fighters.

Known as the 'King of B-29 Killers', Isamu Kashiide's name became well known in the JAAF during the latter part of the home defence campaign. Born in 1915 in Niigata Prefecture, the young Kashiide's boyhood dream of becoming a fighter pilot became a reality when he entered aviation school in February 1934. He graduated in November of the following year, and then joined the 1st Air Regiment.

In July 1938 Kashiide was assigned to the 59th Sentai in northern China, but by the time he arrived in-theatre there was no opportunity for him to experience action against the Chinese Air Force. However, in September of the following year his Ki-27-equipped unit went to Nomonhan, and this time he saw enough combat to make up for the disappointment of the year before. On the very last day of fighting he became involved in a mêlée with eight I-16s and managed to shoot down two of his assailants, although he was nearly shot down himself. At the end of the Nomonhan Incident, Kashiide returned to Hankow, in central China, with seven victories to his credit.

He was assigned to the Formosa-based 4th Sentai in the spring of 1940, and the outbreak of the Pacific War found him performing air defence duties in obsolescent Ki-27s. Within weeks his unit was taking part in the invasion of the Philippines, although the sentai returned to Kozuki Airfield, in Japan, before Kashiide could add to his victory tally.

The 4th Sentai was equipped with the Ki-45 *Toryu* in mid-1943, but the twin-engined fighter escort soon proved to be ill-suited to its designated role. However, when outfitted with a 37 mm cannon in the nose and rear-upward firing 20 mm weapons in the fuselage, the Kawasaki type indeed metamorphosed into a 'Dragon Slayer'.

On the night of 15-16 June 1944, China-based B-29s commenced their first attacks on the Japanese homeland. Their mission was to destroy the Imperial Steel and Iron Works at Yawata, and opposing them was 1Lt Kashiide and his squadron, amongst other JAAF units. Once the resulting interception was over, he reported having shot down two bombers, and was uncertain about the fate of a third. Kashiide followed up this success on 20 August, when he claimed three B-29s shot down and a further trio damaged during a daylight raid.

He soon developed his own style of combat through countless encounters with the Superfortresses, and drilled his subordinates hard in his unique teachings. Years after the war had ended, Kashiide recalled the following instructions;

'Manoeuvre from within 1000 metres. The B-29s have 13 machine guns – in a head-on attack, you will be faced by 10 of them. I will always fly in front and I will always be the first to attack. I am showered with tracers every time. Tracers coming toward you in a criss-cross pattern are very frightening. I feel that my vision is shot away in the screen of bullets. It is not a good feeling to have. In such cases, close your eyes and count to three. When you open your eyes, the enemy will be within 200 metres of you. Adjust your sight to within 150 to 200 metres of the target. At 100 metres, lower your aeroplane. At 80 metres, fire, then dive your aeroplane quickly – go straight down.'

On 27 January 1945 Kashiide shot down a B-29 of the 878th BS/499th BG over Tokyo, a 37 mm round hitting 'T-27' *Rover Boys Express* squarely in the nose. For distinguished service against hordes of B-29s, 1Lt Kashiide received the Bukosho on 8 May 1945 from Lt Gen Isamu Yokoyama. His citation read;

'This distinguished person, on 27 March 1945, at the time of the assault of northern Kyushu by American Air Force B-29s over the air of the protected area, carried out his daredevil attack, shooting down three B-29s and damaging others, and achieved this glorious result. His actions were based on severe fighting spirit and techniques which enabled him to defeat many enemy aeroplanes. His feat glorifies the spirit of the Imperial Army combat squadrons. His military record is outstanding. Therefore, he is hereby awarded the Bukosho B Class.'

By war's end Kashiide had claimed to have destroyed 26 B-29s over Japan, plus of course the seven Soviet fighters he had shot down at Nomonhan. His score is widely disputed by historians and former pilots alike, and today it is believed that he scored no more than seven B-29s, plus two fighters in 1939. Even if this were true, it was still an incredible accomplishment, since most JAAF pilots agreed that it was almost an impossible task for a single pilot to bring down a B-29.

Kashiide was also an eyewitness to the beginning of the atomic age, for he viewed the nuclear destruction of Hiroshima and Nagasaki from the air.

On 17 September 1985 Capt Kashiide met Raymond F 'Hap' Halloran, the navigator aboard *Rover Boys Express* which he had shot down over 40 years before. They shook hands in the spirit of friendship brought by decades of peace, and marvelled at how they had both survived the war.

9

Ki-61-I-Tei of the 244th Sentai *Shinten Seiku Tai*, flown by section leader Lt Tohru Shinomiya, Chofu airfield, December 1944
Unlike other air-to-air ramming sections, which totally

121

stripped their fighters of guns, the 244th kept its Ki-61s fully armed. Adopting an all-red tail marking, the unit further personalised its 'Tonys' by adding the first syllable of the pilot's surname phonetically in white paint onto the rudder. In this case, the lettering (barely visible) represents the sound 'shi' in Shinomiya. A section of this aircraft's left wing was lost in a ramming attack on 3 December 1944 over Tokyo, although Shinomiya still succeeded in landing safely back at Chofu – he was awarded the Bukosho for this exploit. On 29 April 1945, Lt Shinomiya was killed on Okinawa while leading a suicide attack. He was posthumously promoted to major.

10

Ki-61-I-KAIc No 3024 of the 244th Sentai, flown by Group CO Capt Teruhiko Kobayashi, Chofu airfield, late January 1945

Teruhiko Kobayashi became a dashing hero in the latter part of the Japanese home defence. Born in 1920, he had entered the Army Military Academy in the late 1930s and graduated in the 53rd Class. Initially appointed as a second lieutenant in the artillery, Kobayashi soon changed courses to light bombers, and was assigned to the 45th Sentai upon graduation.

On the opening day of the Pacific War he participated in the bombing of Hong Kong, and by April 1943 had become a seasoned veteran of many operational sorties with the 66th Sentai in Manchuria. When the air group enlarged he decided to convert to fighters, and was posted to the Akeno Fighter School. A promotion to captain came in November 1943, and upon the completion of his course in June 1944, Kobayashi was retained in Japan to serve as education officer with the school.

In the latter part of November 1944 he was made an assistant to the commander of the 244th Sentai, this unit subsequently becoming the darling of the general public as it strove to defend Japan from enemy bombers. Armed with the sleek Ki-61-I-KAI Hien, the sentai provided protection for the Tokyo area from their base at Chofu airfield in the western suburbs of the city.

At the age of 24, Capt Kobayashi became the youngest air group commander in the JAAF, leading the sentai by example. His unit gained considerable fame against the B-29s, and by war's end the 244th Sentai could boast a number of successful Superfortress hunters.

Kobayashi himself shot down a B-29 in a single pass on 3 December 1944, while his group claimed six additional aircraft on the same sortie through ramming attacks (all the pilots survived). On 22 December he damaged a B-29 over Akumihan Island, and then on 9 January he damaged another Superfortress, although on this occasion his Hien was hit by return fire and he was forced to make an emergency landing. Eighteen days later Kobayashi destroyed a B-29 through ramming, escaping death by taking to his parachute – his only injury was a slight cut on the bridge of his nose.

The exploits of the 244th Sentai were published daily in newspapers at the time, and Kobayashi's fame continued to grow. On 12 April he damaged yet another B-29, but was wounded in the leg by return fire and forced to take to his parachute once again. The following month his unit received a letter of commendation from the Army High Command, and at the same time his deeds were recognised by the award of the Bukosho.

On 25 July Maj Kobayashi disobeyed orders by taking off to intercept marauding Hellcats over Yokaichi airfield, having been instructed to stay on the ground to await incoming bombers. He and his men were by this late stage in the war flying the superlative Kawasaki Ki-100 Goshikisen (Type 5 Fighter), and in the dogfight that took place at hangar-top height, the 244th Sentai pilots reportedly shot down ten of the VF-31 Hellcats that had sortied over Japan from the carrier USS Belleau Wood – the real score was just two for two on both sides.

Newspapers trumpeted the rout, but a court martial was planned for the young commander, which carried a very serious penalty. However, news of his great deed reached the Emperor, and words of Imperial approval were spoken in respect to Kobayashi's actions – the court martial was quickly dropped.

Maj Kobayashi scored five victories in total (three B-29s and two F6F Hellcats), although post-war Japanese historians have erroneously credited him with ten B-29s and two fighters. This latter score, which would have made him the top JAAF B-29 hunter, is based on self-serving statements by Kobayashi's widow, and photos showing numerous victory markings on his aircraft. Extensive investigation by Japanese historian Takashi Sakurai has subsequently shown that the lower score is correct.

After the war, Kobayashi joined the Self-Defense Air Force, but on 4 June 1957 he was killed in a training accident when the T-33 he was flying crashed on approach to landing at Hamamatsu Air Base in bad weather. He had earlier ordered his subordinate to eject from the aircraft when it had developed a technical problem in flight. Teruhiko Kobayashi remained a hero to the end.

This particular Hien was one of several flown by the charismatic Kobayashi during his numerous home defence missions, and it features four B-29 silhouettes beneath the cockpit to denote his rising tally of claims. Whenever he obtained another aircraft, Kobayashi had his crewchief immediately apply his victory tally to the new fighter. By war's end his final Ki-61 would boast 14 victory markings, a total which also included those aircraft he had simply damaged. Many post-war historians have misinterpreted this total, thus giving Kobayashi credit for downing 14 aircraft, when in reality his final score was five exactly – three B-29s and two Hellcats, plus a further nine Superfortresses damaged.

11

Ki-61-I-KAIc No 3295 of the 244th Sentai, flown by Group CO Capt Teruhiko Kobayashi, Chofu airfield, late January 1945

Operated concurrently with No 3024 (the subject of the previous profile) by Teruhiko Kobayashi, No 3295 was used by the ace to ram a B-29 at 30,000 ft over Mt Fuji on 27 January 1945. He safely parachuted from the stricken Hien, having suffered the smallest of cuts across the bridge of his nose.

12

Ki-61-I-KAIc of HQ flight/244th Sentai, flown by T/Sgt Kiyoshi Ando, Chofu airfield, late January 1945

Whilst serving as wingman for Capt Kobayashi, Kiyoshi Ando also rammed a B-29 (42-63541 Ghastly Goose of the 497th BG, piloted by Capt Dale Peterson) over Mt Fuji on

27 January. However, unlike his leader, Ando died in the collision, crashing with his shattered fighter at Funabashi, in Chiba prefecture, on the north side of Tokyo Bay.

13

Ki-61-I-Hei of the 244th Sentai, flown by Sgt Masao Itagaki, Chofu airfield, January 1945
Masao Itagaki belonged to a B-29 ramming squadron called the Shinten Seiku Tai. The white phonetic katakana character on the tail is the 'ee' in Itagaki. On 3 December 1944 Cpl Itagaki rammed and damaged a B-29 of the 498th BG ('T-49' *Long Distance*) over Tokyo, and managed to parachute to safety – he won the Bukosho for the attack. On 27 January 1945, he rammed another B-29 and again escaped by parachute to win his second Bukosho. From March to May, Itagaki flew *kamikaze* escort missions to Okinawa. He survived the war as one of only two known double Bukosho recipients.

14

Ki-61-I-Hei of the 18th Sentai/6th Shinten Seiku Tai, flown by 1Lt Mitsuo Oyake, Kashiwa airfield, January 1945
The Ki-61 'Tony' was considered to be one of the best B-29 destroyers thanks to its superior diving speed. The type had a service ceiling of 10,000 m (32,810 ft) and a maximum speed of 590 kmh at 4260 m (366 mph at 13,980 ft). 1Lt Mitsuo Oyake flew this fighter with the 18th Sentai during the early months of 1945. On 7 April he attacked a B-29 repeatedly but failed to bring it down, so he finally resorted to ramming. With its tail lost, the B-29 fell at Kugayama (Suginami Ward, Tokyo). Oyake bailed out, lost consciousness and landed in a tree, but survived. He continued to fight until the day the war ended, claiming four B-29s destroyed and three damaged. Oyake also received the Bukosho for outstanding service.

15

Ki-84-Ko of the 3rd Chutai/103rd Sentai, flown by 1Lt Shigeyasu Miyamoto, Itami airfield, January 1945
Shigeyasu Miyamoto's first combat came in January 1945 when he intercepted B-29s over Japan. On 15 April he led eight fighters on a bombing raid against the north airfield on Okinawa, and on his return had to fight off the attention of an F6F-5 Hellcat. Miyamoto was wounded in the engagement, and was forced to make an emergency landing in his 'Frank' on Tokuno Island. He won the Bukosho on 4 May for heroism during the Okinawan battles, and survived the war.

16

Ki-45-KAI of the 2nd Chutai/4th Sentai, flown by WO Sadamitsu Kimura, Kozuki airfield, January 1945
This aircraft has a pair of obliquely-mounted (at an angle of 70 degrees) Ho-5 20 mm cannon fitted in place of the 59 Imp gal upper fuselage tank. This arrangement was put to deadly use by Sadamitsu Kimura, who claimed 22 B-29s destroyed before he was shot down and killed by Superfortress gunners on the night of 13-14 July 1945.

One of the top JAAF bomber hunters, Kimura was born in Chiba Prefecture on 19 August 1915. By May 1938 he had entered flight training, and was assigned to the 4th Sentai in 1942. Kimura's entire war career centred around home defence duties and fighting B-29s. When the Boeing bombers first raided Japan on the night of 15-16 June

1944, Kimura took off in his Ki-45 from Kozuki Airfield to intercept them, and by the time he returned had claimed two B-29s shot down and three damaged. This was his unit's first major success of the war, and Kimura was duly awarded a ceremonial sword. He also received a personal citation from Gen Shimomura of the Western Military District.

On 27 March 1945 Kimura flew three missions during the night and claimed an incredible five B-29s shot down, with a further two damaged. On 1 May he was awarded the Bukosho for distinguished service. On the night of 13-14 July 1945, 313rd BW B-29s mined the Shimonoseki Straits, and Kimura reported by radio that he had damaged a Superfortress and was going in to finish the stricken bomber off – this was his last transmission.

Capt Isamu Kashiide, another great B-29 hunter and a squadronmate of Kimura's, wrote in his post-war memoirs that the latter had shot down some 22 B-29s. Japanese historians have attributed him with eight victories, however.

17

Ki-45-KAI of the 53rd Sentai Shinten *Seiku Tai*, Matsudo airfield, February 1945
This particular Ki-45 served with the air-to-air suicide unit attached to the Shinten Seiku Tai (Shinten Intercept Unit) air group. The arrow marking on the fighter's fuselage was inspired by the *Kabura-ya*, this insignia having originally served as the personal motif of Kusunoki Masashige, a great feudal warrior of ancient Japan. Thanks to its distinctive perforated design (note its turnip-shaped head), the *Kabura-ya* made a sound in flight when shot off, and it was traditionally fired into the air as a signal to commence combat. Since this Ki-45-KAI was exclusively employed as a ramming aircraft, the rear observer's position was done away with, and the rear cockpit faired over with sheet metal.

18

Ki-84-Ko of the 51st Sentai, flown by Capt Tadao Ikeda, Shimodate airfield, February 1945
The 51st Sentai returned from the Philippines for home defence duties in November 1944, Capt Tadao Ikeda in turn arriving from Manchuria to assume command of the air group. He organised four to six-aircraft formations of well-trained pilots as a nucleus for the younger novice pilots. On 16 February 1945, Capt Ikeda led five fighters against 20 Hellcats of VBF-12 that were strafing Hokota army airfield. Ikeda and M/Sgt Kawamura claimed one F6F apiece, and all six 'Franks' returned to base – two Japanese fighters suffered minor battle damage. The unit enjoyed little success against the B-29s.

19

Ki-61-I-Hei of the 39th Educational Squadron, flown by M/Sgt Iwao Tabata, Yokoshiba airfield, March 1945
M/Sgt Iwao Tabata was a seasoned combat veteran who had served with the 68th Sentai in New Guinea. Shot down and wounded over Wewak, he returned home to become an instructor with the 39th Educational Squadron. When the bombing raids on the home islands commenced, Tabata also participated in air defence operations against B-29s. This 'Tony' is adorned with four victory markings, the two small stylised wings representing

fighters the veteran instructor had shot down and the silhouettes of two bombers denoting B-29 victories. The squadron's tail insignia is a stylised *kanji* '39'.

20

Ki-61-I-Tei of the 56th Sentai, Itami airfield, March 1945
The 55th and 56th Sentais were formed at the same time, at Taisho airfield, in March 1944. Both purely home defence units armed exclusively with the Ki-61, the latter sentai was led by Maj Haruyoshi Furukawa. He duly led the 56th from its inception until the end of the war, the unit being officially credited with 11 B-29 victories at the cost of 30 pilots. Maj Furukawa explained to the authors that the unit's emblem was designed by a groundcrewman.

21

Ki-45-KAI-Ko of the 3rd Chutai/5th Sentai, flown by Chutai CO Capt Fujitaro Ito, Kiyosu airfield, March 1945
Totaro Ito used this aircraft to destroy the bulk of his 13 bomber kills, a tally which included no less than nine B-29s – understandably, he was awarded a Bukosho for his feats in combat. The white *kanji* characters on the tail reads 'Kuzuryu', which was a nine-headed dragon in Japanese mythology.

Although a relative unknown when compared to the more famous B-29 hunters profiled in this volume, Capt Fujitaro Ito may just be the top four-engined bomber destroyer of the entire JAAF. Born in 1916 in Fukui Prefecture, he enlisted in the Army in the mid-1930s and initially served in the 36th Infantry Regiment. In April 1939 he entered the NCO flight training course, and duly graduated from Kumagaya Flying School in December. Ito was then posted to the 5th Sentai, a unit with which he stayed until war's end.

Having seen several years of frontline service with this sentai, Ito then entered the Aviation Commissioned Officers' Academy as a candidate for second lieutenant in June 1942. He graduated in November of that same year, and three months later received his commission.

In July 1943 Ito departed with his unit for duty south of Java, and was engaged in various combats. By 19 January 1944 the 5th Sentai was based at Rian airfield, on Ambon Island, in the East Indies. The unit had been equipped with the Ki-45 prior to deploying to Rian, thus becoming the first sentai in the JAAF to receive the new heavy fighter.

Ito's first combat with the 'Dragon Slayer' occurred soon after his arrival in the East Indies, his chutai responding to a surprise raid staged by a formation of B-24s on the airfield. Seven Liberators fell to the heavily-armed Ki-45s, three of them to 2Lt Ito and his observer, Sgt Masanori Nozaki. They had taken on a four-bomber formation, and quickly despatched a trio of B-24s using the fighter's 37 mm cannon. Their own aircraft was hit in the right engine, however, and they were forced to make an emergency landing at Seramu Island. Due to the bravery shown in the face of overwhelming odds, both Ito and Nozaki received personal commendations from Gen Tsukuda, the regional air commander.

In mid-May 1944, Ito and Nozaki again encountered enemy bombers, but this time their 'Nick' was hit before they could inflict any damage on the formation. They were forced to make an emergency landing in the sea, but were quickly rescued. Ito later flew air defence patrols around Nanking before returning to Japan.

In December 1944 Marianas-based B-29s started to attack Nagoya, and the recently-promoted 1Lt Ito was in the vanguard thrown up by the JAAF in an attempt to thwart their efforts. Over the next eight months he would tackle USAAF bombers in Ki-45s, Ki-61s and finally Ki-100s. In January 1945 he took control of the 3rd Chutai, and proceeded to lead it until the end of the war – he had shot down more than nine B-29s by VJ-Day. In light of his efforts in the final desperate months of war, Ito was awarded the Bukosho on 7 July 1945. Capt Ito shot down more than 13 enemy aircraft, all of which were bombers. He passed away on 15 May 1983.

22

Ki-61-I-Tei of the 55th Sentai, Sano airfield, late March 1945
The 55th Sentai, armed exclusively with the Ki-61 'Tony', was formed at Taisho airfield in March 1944. As part of the 18th Fighter Division, its main duty was home defence. Having briefly seen action in the Philippines in late 1944, the unit achieved no spectacular results whilst defending Japan. Aircraft 37 was based at Sano, on the eastern coast of Osaka Bay south-west of Osaka city.

23

Ki-61-I-KAIc of the 244th Sentai, flown by Group CO Capt Teruhiko Kobayashi, Chofu airfield, April 1945
Yet another Ki-61 associated with Teruhiko Kobayashi, this aircraft may have been the *Hien* he bailed out of on 12 April 1945 after it was badly shot up by B-29 gunners during an attacking pass. Due to the intense media interest in the exploits of the 244th Sentai, Kobayashi always ensured that every aircraft he flew reflected the success of 'his' unit.

24

Ki-61-I-KAIc No 3024 of the 244th Sentai, flown by Group CO Capt Teruhiko Kobayashi, Chofu airfield, April 1945
This profile again depicts No 3024 (see profile 10) but at a later date, with ten B-29 silhouettes and a pair of Hellcats detailed beneath the cockpit. Kobayashi's sixth kill is further embellished with a red Ki-61 sprayed over the white planform of a B-29 – this elaborate marking denoted the Mt Fuji ramming attack. To instill morale in his pilots, the sentai leader had the word *Hissho* ('confidence of victory') emblazoned on the rudder of his fighter in white paint.

25

Ki-45-KAI-Hei of the 4th Sentai/*Kaiten Tai*, flown by Lt Miosaburo Yamamoto, Kozuki airfield, April 1945
Miosaburo Yamamoto has had his surname written in Japanese phonetics on the tail of this Ki-45, which was common practice amongst suicide pilots. Yamamoto was killed in this machine during a ramming attack on a B-29 over Fukuoka Prefecture on 18 April 1945.

26

Ki-84-Ko of the Army Flight Test Centre, flown by M/Sgt Isamu Sasaki, Fussa airfield, May 1945
Unlike many of the more famous JAAF fighter pilots of World War 2, Isamu Sasaki's extraordinary accomplishments have received very little recognition over the years. Born in 1921 in Hiroshima Prefecture, he left technical school and joined the Tokyo Army Aviation

School in April 1938. Upon graduation in March 1941, he was assigned to the 50th Sentai, based on Formosa.

On the first day of the Pacific War Sasaki took part in the invasion of the Philippines, his baptism of fire taking place on 10 December 1941 over Bigan Bay when he chased a B-17C that had made a surprise attack on the Japanese invasion fleet. He pursued the Boeing bomber towards the vicinity of Bagio, where Navy Zero fighters took over the hunt.

In January 1942 Sasaki advanced into Thailand with his unit and scored his first victory over Rangoon. In the violent Burma campaign he went on to achieve over 20 kills against fighters, as well as claiming he have destroyed more than a dozen larger aircraft. In April 1944 he returned to Japan to become an examiner of test pilots.

Sasaki's courage and elaborate skills were aptly demonstrated to the examination department on 25 May 1945 when, in a single night action against B-29s over Tokyo, he targeted the enemy by silhouetting them against the great fires below. He would then dive at his victim head-on – he shot down three Superfortresses in this fashion in a matter of minutes.

By the end of hostilities, Sasaki had destroyed six B-29s (three on the night of 25 May 1945 while flying this aircraft) and damaged three others, bringing his total war claims to at least 38. For his actions against B-29s, allied with his distinguished record in Burma, Sasaki was awarded the Bukosho (Medal of Honour, B Class) and received a promotion to warrant officer.

After the war, Sasaki changed his name to Hirayama and joined the Japan Self-Defence Air Force. He is now retired, and resides in Hiroshima Prefecture.

27
Ki-100-I of the 59th Sentai, Ashiya airfield, May 1945
This aircraft belonged to the 3rd Chutai, commanded by 1Lt Naoyuki Ogata, who led the unit from April 1945 until the end of the war. The poor quality of aircraft paint has contributed to the fighter's excessively weathered appearance. The *Goshikisen* was basically a Ki-61 airframe fitted with a 1500 hp Mitsubishi Ha-112-II air-cooled radial engine in place of the Kawasaki inline, liquid-cooled Ha-140 (a licence-built Daimler-Benz DB 601A), rated at the same horsepower. The combination proved outstanding, for the fighter could more than hold its own against the Hellcat and Mustang, and proved very capable of intercepting B-29s at high altitude. Most Japanese pilots considered the Ki-100 to have been the best JAAF fighter of the war.

28
Ki-100-I-Otsu of the 5th Sentai, Kiyosu airfield, June 1945
Considered the 'best of the best', the Otsu variant of the excellent Ki-100 was in production from May to July 1945. Hastily assembled, fighters were sprayed at the factory in the standard green finish on the fuselage and upper-surfaces, while the undersides remained unpainted. Known simply as the *Goshikisen* (Type 5 fighter), the Ki-100 proved easy to master, and was the ideal platform for intercepting both B-29s and their Mustang escorts. The 5th Sentai, which defended the Nagoya area from December 1944 until the end of the war, received its first Ki-100s in May 1945. By VJ-Day the sentai had claimed 40 B-29s destroyed for the loss of just 16 pilots.

29
Ki-45-KAI of the 2nd Chutai/4th Sentai, flown by Lt Hannoshin Nishio, Kozuki airfield, June 1945
The *kanji* writing on the rear fuselage of this Ki-45 denotes that it was a donated aircraft that had been purchased for the JAAF by an organisation in Yamaguchi Prefecture, near to where the 4th Sentai was based. Its regular pilot, Hannoshin Nishio, downed at least five B-29s in the final months of the war.

30
Ki-44-II-Hei of the 3rd Chutai/70th Sentai, flown by Capt Yoshio Yoshida, Kashiwa airfield, June 1945
This was the personal aircraft of Yoshio Yoshida, who commanded the chutai from February 1945 until war's end. One of the top B-29 hunters of the JAAF, he was born in 1921 in Hiroshima City, entered the 55th Class of the Army Officers' Flight Academy in 1939, and upon graduation in March 1942 was sent to the Akeno Fighter School for additional training, prior to being posted to the 70th Sentai.

When the USAAF's XX Bomber Command sent 96 B-29s to attack targets in Anshan, Manchuria, for the first time on 29 July 1944, the 70th Sentai was transferred into the region the following month so as to provide some form of defence for the Japanese colonial territory. The air group was equipped with the Ki-44-II-Hei.

On 8 September a force of 108 B-29s raided Anshan for a second time, and in the subsequent engagement between the Superfortresses and the 'Tojos', 1Lt Yoshida managed to claim one as a probable.

The thundering hordes of B-29s started to raid the Tokyo region in November 1944, and in an attempt to counter the menace, the 70th Sentai was transferred back to Kashiwa Airfield, near the capital, where it swapped its near-useless 'Tojos' for the far superior Ki-84 'Frank'. Yoshida was given command of the 3rd Chutai in February 1945, and he immediately began to hone his attacks against the four-engined bombers. On 13 April he shot down a B-29, followed by another two days later. By 25 May Yoshida had increased his tally to six Superfortresses destroyed and one probable following a series of successful night actions – all of these are marked, with appropriate dates, on the side of this fighter. The second-highest scoring B-29 hunter of the 70th Sentai, Yoshida was awarded the Bukosho as a result of his extraordinary successes in the obsolescent 'Tojo'.

31
Ki-84-Ko of the 246th Sentai, flown by WO Kenji Fujimoto, Taisho airfield, July 1945
This aircraft was flown by Kenji Fujimoto, who destroyed three B-29s (two by ramming on 13 and 16 March 1945) and duly won the Bukosho. He was shot down and killed by P-47Ns near Lake Biwa (north of Kyoto) on 14 August 1945 – just 24 hours before the cessation of hostilities.

32
Ki-44-II-Hei of the 3rd Chutai/70th Sentai, flown by 2Lt Makoto Ogawa, Kashiwa airfield, June 1945
This weary combat veteran was the personal mount of Makoto Ogawa, who preferred to record his B-29 victories using stylised eagles. As the leading B-29 hunter of the 70th Sentai, he downed seven Superfortresses and two Mustangs.

Ogawa was born in 1917 in Shizuoka Prefecture. He joined the 7th Air Regiment at Hamamatsu in 1935, and eventually transferred over to fighters. In August 1938 Ogawa graduated from the Kumagaya Aviation School in the 72nd term class, and instead of being posted to a frontline unit, he was employed as an assistant flight instructor at his old school. Finally, in late 1941, he was transferred to Manchuria to serve with the 70th Sentai.

For the first three years of the Pacific War the 70th Sentai fulfilled the air defence role for the northern extremities of Manchuria, but in the autumn of 1944 it was brought back to defend Tokyo – the unit re-equipped with Ki-84s to perform this task. After more than seven solid years as a pilot, Ogawa had attained a high level of proficiency, and during night operations against B-29s, he quickly developed a method of frontal assaults. During daylight missions, however, Ogawa would only commence his attack once the bombers had started to drop their load, as the B-29 pilots would be forced to maintain level flight during the release. This made them easy targets for Ogawa, and he downed two Superfortresses using this method of attack.

By war's end he had destroyed seven B-29s and two P-51Ds, a score which made Ogawa the leading ace of the 70th Sentai. On 9 July 1945 he was awarded the Bukosho by Gen Seiichi Tanaka, and promoted to second lieutenant.

33

Ki-100-I-Ko of the 3rd Chutai/59th Sentai, flown by Chutai CO 1Lt Naoyuki Ogata, Ashiya airfield, August 1945
Only 272 examples of the Ki-100-I-Ko were produced between February and June 1945, and this variant accounted for most of the production run of the superlative Kawasaki fighter. The pilot of this particular aircraft, 1Lt Naoyuki Ogata, had served as a Ki-61 instructor at the Akeno Fighter School prior to his assignment to the 59th Sentai. On 15 August 1944, when China-based B-29s attacked northern Kyushu for the first time, Ogata claimed three bombers shot down. He was subsequently credited with destroying an F6F Hellcat on 14 May 1945 over Sakura Island, and his fifth, and final victory (a P-51D) was achieved on 14 August 1945 over Ashiya airfield. Ogata was awarded the Bukosho for distinguished service in the final weeks of the war.

34

Ki-61-I-Tei of the 244th Sentai, Chofu airfield, August 1945
A photograph of this unusually marked aircraft was taken by an American officer of the occupation force at the end of the war. Featuring 12 victory markings in the form of four-engined bombers (B-29s?) on its nose, the fighter is believed to have been the final mount of unit CO, Capt Teruhiko Kobayashi. Whenever he changed aircraft, he had his mechanic transfer the victory markings to his new aircraft. The fighter may have also been flown by Capt Chuichi Ichikawa, who claimed nine B-29s and a Hellcat shot down, and a further six Boeing bombers damaged – this success saw him awarded the Bukosho. The most unusual marking on this Ki-61 is undoubtedly its green-leafed clover behind the cockpit. The clover, or shamrock, had no symbolic significance to the Japanese, although to the Americans it meant good luck. Therefore, it may well have been the handiwork of a bored GI with too much time on his hands!

BIBLIOGRAPHY

Campbell, J M. *Boeing B-29 Superfortress*. Schiffer Publishing, 1997

Birdsall, S. *Saga Of The Superfortress*. Doubleday & Co, 1980

Bradley, F J. *No Strategic Targets Left*. Turner Publishing, 1999

Fukubayashi, T. *Hondo Kushu No Tsuiraku Beigunki To Horyo Hikoshi (American planes downed and airmen captured during air raids on Japan)*. Privately published, Kyoto, 2000

Harada, R. *Nihon Daikushu (Mass air raids on Japan)*. Chuo-Koronsha Publishers, Tokyo, 1973

Hata, I. *Dainji Taisen Koku Shiwa (Aviation episodes in World War 2)*. Kofusha Publishers, Tokyo, 1986

Hata, I and Izawa, Y. *Nihon Rikugun Sento Tai (Japanese Army fighter units)*. Kantosha Publishers, Tokyo, 1977

Kashiide, I. *B-29 Gekitsui Ki (A memoir about destroying B-29s)*. Kojinsha Publishers, Tokyo, 1998

Marshall, C. *Sky Giants Over Japan*. Global Press, 1984

Marshall, C. *The Global Twentieth*. Marshall Publishers, 1985

Rust, K C. *Twentieth Air Force Story*. Historical Aviation Album, 1979

Watanabe, Y. *Hondo Bokusen (The home defence air battle)*. Asahi Sonorama Publishers, 1982

Watanabe, Y. *Rikugun Boku Sen (Japanese air defence, pictorial history of the air war over Japan, Japanese Army Air Force)*. Hara Shobo Co, 1980

Watanabe, Y. Japanese translation of *Superfortress: The B-29 And American Power* by C E LeMay and B Yenne. Asahi Sonorama Publishers, Tokyo, 1991

Yamamoto, S. *B-29 Tai Rikugun Sento Tai (B-29s versus Japanese Army fighters)*. Konnichi No Wadaisha Publishers, Tokyo, 1973

INDEX

References to illustrations are shown in **bold**. Colour Plates are prefixed 'pl.', with page and caption locators in brackets.